Editor-in-Chief and Founder:
  Lyndon H. LaRouche, Jr.
Editorial Board: *Lyndon H. LaRouche, Jr. , Helga
  Zepp-LaRouche, Robert Ingraham, Tony
  Papert, Gerald Rose, Dennis Small, Jeffrey
  Steinberg, William Wertz*
Co-Editors: *Robert Ingraham, Tony Papert*
Technology: *Marsha Freeman*
Transcriptions: *Katherine Notley*
Ebooks: *Richard Burden*
Graphics: *Alan Yue*
Photos: *Stuart Lewis*
Circulation Manager: *Stanley Ezrol*

INTELLIGENCE DIRECTORS
Economics: *Marcia Merry Baker, Paul Gallagher*
History: *Anton Chaitkin*
Ibero-America: *Dennis Small*
Russia and Eastern Europe: *Rachel Douglas*
United States: *Debra Freeman*

INTERNATIONAL BUREAUS
Bogotá: *Miriam Redondo*
Berlin: *Rainer Apel*
Copenhagen: *Tom Gillesberg*
Lima: *Sara Madueño*
Melbourne: *Robert Barwick*
Mexico City: *Gerardo Castilleja Chávez*
New Delhi: *Ramtanu Maitra*
Paris: *Christine Bierre*
Stockholm: *Ulf Sandmark*
United Nations, N.Y.C.: *Leni Rubinstein*
Washington, D.C.: *William Jones*
Wiesbaden: *Göran Haglund*

ON THE WEB
e-mail: eirns@larouchepub.com
www.larouchepub.com
www.executiveintelligencereview.com
www.larouchepub.com/eiw
Webmaster: *John Sigerson*
Assistant Webmaster: *George Hollis*
Editor, Arabic-language edition: *Hussein Askary*

EIR (ISSN 0273-6314) *is published weekly
(50 issues), by EIR News Service, Inc.,
P.O. Box 17390, Washington, D.C. 20041-0390.
(703) 297-8434*

European Headquarters: E.I.R. GmbH, Postfach
Bahnstrasse 9a, D-65205, Wiesbaden, Germany
Tel: 49-611-73650
Homepage: http://www.eir.de
e-mail: info@eir.de
Director: Georg Neudecker

Montreal, Canada: 514-461-1557
eir@eircanada.ca

Denmark: EIR - Danmark, Sankt Knuds Vej 11,
basement left, DK-1903 Frederiksberg, Denmark.
Tel.: +45 35 43 60 40, Fax: +45 35 43 87 57. e-mail:
eirdk@hotmail.com.

Mexico City: EIR, Sor Juana Inés de la Cruz 242-2
Col. Agricultura C.P. 11360
Delegación M. Hidalgo, México D.F.
Tel. (5525) 5318-2301
eirmexico@gmail.com

Copyright: ©2018 EIR News Service. All rights
reserved. Reproduction in whole or in part without
permission strictly prohibited.

Canada Post Publication Sales Agreement
#40683579

Postmaster: Send all address changes to *EIR*, P.O.
Box 17390, Washington, D.C. 20041-0390.

Signed articles in *EIR* represent the views of the authors,
and not necessarily those of the Editorial Board.

A New Beginning

EU SUMMIT MUST FOLLOW SINGAPORE EXAMPLE!

History Is Now Being Written in Asia!

by Helga Zepp-LaRouche, chairwoman of the German political party
Civil Rights Movement Solidarity (*BüSo*)

June 15—The contrast could hardly be clearer. In Singapore, the historic summit between President Donald Trump and Chairman Kim Jong-un launched a process that, beyond the region itself, could guarantee world peace for the future; at the same time, the Shanghai Cooperation Organization (SCO) rang in a new era in building a new world order based on trust, harmony and joint development. On the other hand, there was the disunited, antagonistic G-7 summit, whose European heads of state and government then *returned home*, only to plunge into a new dispute over the flare-up of the refugee crisis, and to react to that crisis with remedies as heinous as they are useless. It is high time for a policy reorientation on the old continent! The immediate opportunity to do so is the upcoming EU summit on June 28-29!

Notwithstanding all the cynical comments from the usual suspects in the mainstream media, the groundbreaking summit between Trump and Kim Jong-un would never have been possible without the spirit of the New Silk Road, which has swept over Asia in particular in recent years. Indeed, the idea of economically including North Korea in the integration of China's Belt and Road Initiative and the Eurasian Economic Union was very much present at last year's Eastern Economic Forum in Vladivostok. And at the Panmunjom Inter-Korean summit in April of this year, South Korean President Moon Jae-in presented his North Korean counterpart with a USB thumb drive containing detailed plans for the economic development of the North.

The White House, in collaboration with the National Security Council, had prepared a video envisaging the perspective of a modern, industrialized, prosperous North Korea—a high-speed rail system, a Chinese maglev, industrial parks, a country on the rise—which Trump showed the North Korean Chairman during their meeting before the final press conference. I recommend to those in the West, whose minds have been herded like cattle into brand identities and stuffed full of prejudices, by the media, that they watch Trump's press conference themselves. A sovereign U.S. President presented the outcome of the summit: the total nuclear disarmament of North Korea, in return for security guarantees, the lifting of sanctions and the pledge to make North Korea prosperous. In addition, he announced the immediate end of the U.S.-South Korean military maneuvers, which he called provocative, saying, "Under the circumstances, we are negotiating a comprehensive and complete deal. It is inappropriate to have war games. Number one, we save money. A lot. Number two, it is really something they very much appreciated."

The people of both Koreas reacted ecstatically to the live broadcast of the Summit and the press conference. President Moon repeatedly commented with enthusiastic applause. We in Germany should recall the elation at the time of the fall of the Berlin Wall to get a sense of the effect on the population there.

Not only did China and Russia in particular conduct important background negotiations with North Korea in the run-up to the summit, but the Russian government has also pledged to assist in economic development, while the Chinese government promised to help provide security guarantees for North Korea. Russian Foreign Minister Sergey Lavrov stressed the importance of resuming the six-party talks for an internationally secured implementation of the agreement. China's *Global Times* wrote that the North Korean economy is by no means as dilapidated as is often assumed: "North Korea has economic and geographic advantages to join the B&R, which will help the country realize its economic potential. It won't be easy, and it won't happen overnight. However, getting North Korea into the B&R initiative to promote economic integration may be easier than what people would have imagined."

How Different the SCO and G-7 Summits!

The almost simultaneous SCO summit, which India and Pakistan attended for the first time as full members, was opened by President Xi Jinping with the greeting that the future will be guided by the spirit of Confucius, whose birthplace is in the same Shandong Province as the conference venue in Qingdao. China's Foreign Minister Wang Yi described the proceedings of the conference as the beginning of a new era in creating an international order based on mutual trust, mutual benefit, equality, respect for diversity and joint development. That, he explained, would transcend the outdated concepts of the clash of civilizations, the Cold War, zero-sum games, or exclusionary clubs.

How different was the G-7 summit in Canada! The photo showing Mrs. Merkel, German Chancellor, in a confrontational attitude toward Trump, surrounded by the other heads of state and government, is likewise an expression of the break-up of the geopolitically oriented post-war order, of the "G-6 against 1" formation. But actually it was only the G-4, because Trump, Japanese Prime Minister Shinzo Abe and Italian Prime Minister Giuseppe Conte do not agree on the continuation of sanctions against Russia. The disunity of the Europeans is clearly visible on the issue of the refugee crisis. It should be obvious to everyone that neither the idea of turning back refugees at the EU's external borders, by whatever method, is practicable, nor will there will be unity in the EU before the upcoming summit on the basis of the "solutions" proposed so far.

German Interior Minister Horst Seehofer's proposal to turn away refugees on the German border, if they are already registered in another EU member country, will tend to lead to the end of the EU's Schengen agreement, and thereby to the destruction of the foundation of the monetary union. The idea of so-called detention camps in countries such as Libya, which has sunk into internal chaos as a result of President Barack Obama's military intervention, is so barbaric that it reduces the oft-cited "western values" once and for all *ad absurdum*.

It is expected that by 2040, two billion people will be living in Africa, a huge part of them young people who need education, a job, and more generally, a perspective for the future. What the African continent needs is massive investment in infrastructure, industrial capacities and agriculture, of precisely the type that China has made in the last ten years. China has thus helped reduce poverty in Africa from 56% in 1990 to 43% in 2012. At the G-20 summit in Hamburg in 2017, Xi Jinping explicitly and repeatedly proposed to Angela Merkel to cooperate with the New Silk Road in Africa. The German government, for its part, has repeatedly spoken of a "Marshall Plan for Africa," but other than the usual green "sustainable" projects, detention camps, and the securing of the EU's external borders, nothing has been forthcoming.

The new Undersecretary of State in the Italian Ministry of Development, Professor Michele Geraci, has just published a memorandum for cooperation between Italy and China, identifying eleven sectors in which Italy has an existential interest to cooperate with China. Among other points, the paper states: "Africa and the migrants? Who can help Africa? China." Geraci reports that China has invested the most in Africa, and thanks to China, poverty in Africa has started to decrease for the first time. "China offers Europe, and Italy in particular, an historical opportunity to cooperate for the social-economic stabilization of Africa, which we should absolutely not miss. Therefore, we must strengthen cooperation between Italy and China in Africa."

This EU Summit Could be Transformative

If the Merkel government is still in place when this article appears, there is a very good way to overcome the present crises—from the migrant crisis to the government crisis and the EU crisis. Taking the example set by the Singapore Summit—that real change is possible, and that the past does not determine the future—the German government should ensure that the agenda of the upcoming European Union summit on June 28-29 be quickly changed. EU cooperation with China's New Silk Road initiative for the development of Africa should be made the sole subject on the agenda, and Xi Jinping or Wang Yi should be invited to attend, as well as some African heads of state who are already cooperating with China.

If the EU summit, the Chinese government representative, and the African representatives then pronounce in a joint declaration the commitment to undertake a joint crash program for a pan-African infrastructure and development program, and promise all the young people of Africa that the continent will overcome poverty in a short time, such a declaration, due to the participation of China, would have all the credibility in the world in Africa, and would change the dynamic in all the countries towards definite hope for the future, and thus would immediately effect a change in the migrant crisis. It would also free the EU from its current crisis of legitimacy, and give the European nations a mission which would place the unity of Europe on a great new level.

Will the heads of state and government of Europe manage to follow the example of Trump and Kim Jong-un? The prospect of developing Africa together with China, would also give President Trump the urgently needed opportunity to overcome the otherwise looming spiral of trade war, and to balance the U.S. trade deficit by increasing trade, primarily through investment in joint ventures in third countries.

The crisis in Europe, the migrant crisis, the crisis of the German government—they have all assumed such dimensions, that the opportunity for a change of course in policy can absolutely be seized. Needed now, are the people to make it happen.

EIR Contents

www.larouchepub.com   Volume 45, Number 25, June 22, 2018

Cover This Week

Chairman Kim and President Trump at the Singapore summit, June 12, 2018.

Rogers Officially Launches Independent Campaign for U.S. Congress in Texas

June 18—On June 6, 2018, the State of Texas put Kesha Rogers on the ballot as an independent candidate for Congress in Texas' 9th C.D. Rogers petitioned for ballot status for the seat presently held by Al "Impeach Trump" Green of Houston. Rogers' run for the seat is based on the simple fact, according to her, that "there is nobody currently in office, or running for office, who is championing any kind of platform to seize the future from the jaws of the failed policy paradigm of the 21st Century." Donald Trump highlighted elements of a possible optimistic future during his campaign, such as the revival of the American System of economics, with its Glass-Steagall protections and domestic industrial productivity. Rogers underscored, "he is essentially a lone voice on the national stage, and often distracted by hand-to-hand combat with 'the swamp': the fake news, British-directed, intelligence and mass media coup against him."

EIRNS

Kesha Rogers in Houston, June 16, 2018.

In her official declaration of intent to run, Rogers noted: "Our nation has been plagued by the continued policies of war and economic collapse, and cultural degeneracy, brought about by a criminal system of looting by Wall Street speculators over decades. This has left several generations of our citizens impoverished, in despair, and overdosing on drugs, with no foreseeable productive future. My commitment is to put an end to such destructive policies by leading a fight to foster the return to the very American System economic principles at the foundation of our nation's Constitution and our republic. I am committed to restoring a productive economy and renewing optimism for our nation, and our prosperity. These needed solutions and the remedies to the continued financial collapse can be found in the Four Economic Laws proposed by statesman and economist Lyndon LaRouche, with whom I have been associated for nearly twenty years."

Rogers won the Democratic nomination in two past campaigns for Congress. In 2010 and 2012 she campaigned on the slogan "Save NASA, Impeach Obama." And in 2014 she became the first person of color in Texas to enter a runoff election for statewide office, running for U.S. Senate, fighting to save the Democratic Party from the train wreck of Obama, and return it to the productive missions of Presidents Franklin Roosevelt and John Kennedy.

Rogers has emphasized that unlike the "petty identity politics and corrupt economic vision" embraced by her opponent, she has an actual economic plan to build massive infrastructure, and to create crash research and development programs on the frontiers of science, starting with the development of fusion power. By reorienting the economy to actual production, rather than the casino economy of recent years, Rogers is focused on creating thousands of high-paying productive jobs.

Specifically, the candidate noted: "I represent a return to the American System of political economy authored by Alexander Hamilton but fundamentally advanced by Lyndon LaRouche's studies of the relationship between increases in technological progress, and increases in the productive powers of human populations," Rogers declared. "La-Rouche's Four Laws call for the crash development of fusion power as the next, revolutionary technology breakthrough, which will jumpstart a new modern infrastructure platform providing the next 50 years (or two generations) of productive employment, including in manned space exploration to the Moon and beyond, a high speed maglev transportation grid, comprehensive water management and flood control systems, and other national investments to increase the standard of living of the population, while advancing the productivity of the economy as a whole.

To facilitate such investment," Rogers explained, "a national commercial banking system must be re-established, with lending authority and interest rates favorable to long term development. This American System must be protected from looting by reinstating Roosevelt's Glass-Steagall law, separating commercial lending from Wall Street's speculative casino activities."

Emancipation for All Humanity

Rogers hosted her official campaign kickoff event at a BBQ restaurant in Missouri City on Juneteenth weekend. Juneteenth recognizes the anniversary of June 19th, 1865, when Union soldiers and Major General Gordon Granger arrived in Texas and announced the

EIRNS

Kesha Rogers campaigning in Missouri City, Texas, June 15, 2018.

total emancipation of all slaves to the people of Galveston, which had actually happened by President Lincoln's proclamation two and a half years earlier. Rogers, in her remarks at that event, proclaimed her sense of hope, saying, "Imagine how enslaved people felt, in the days before and after that announcement. They did not know they had been freed, but they did know the President had been assassinated, and the world seemed hopeless. Then they learned their freedom had already been granted, and even though it took a long time to find out they were free, when they did, they were cheering in the streets.

"This is the same predicament that Americans are experiencing today, on an even greater level. The bankrupt system of economic looting by Wall Street and the British Empire has the world wrapped up in debt slavery and war, and the news of the just world economic order expressed in the Belt and Road Initiative and Lyndon LaRouche's Four Economic Laws has yet to be announced on our shores. People are feeling hopeless, seeing the skyrocketing suicides, opioid overdoses, the coup attempt against the President, and are saddled with so much debt. I am here to bring the news of the way out, and my campaign is dedicated to an emancipation for all humanity."

Forget the Punditry!
The IG's Report Is a Bombshell

by Barbara Boyd

June 15—Today, Department of Justice (DOJ) Inspector General Michael Horowitz released his 565-page report on the FBI and Justice Department's Hillary Clinton email investigation. President Trump and various supporters have expressed outrage that Horowitz did not go further in frying former FBI Director James Comey or declaring the obvious political bias he otherwise documents in the Clinton investigation. These are legitimate issues and there is a legitimate question as to whether Horowitz softened the language in his report because of Justice Department pushback. These issues will be fully explored when the IG testifies in Congressional hearings next week.

Michael Horowitz, DOJ Inspector General.

Nonetheless, the report is a bombshell, even if written in carefully parsed Justice Department lawyer language. If we were not in the middle of an insurrection against the Trump presidency, it would cause an immediate halt to Special Counsel Robert Mueller's investigation.

Proof that the report is a bombshell can be seen in the new-found outrage of Congressman Trey Gowdy, who only a couple weeks back was found cowering under the skirts of House Speaker Paul Ryan as things got hot about British interference in the U.S. election in the form of FBI/MI6 informant Stefan Halper. But in response to the IG report, Gowdy stated, "The report also conclusively shows an alarming and destructive level of animus displayed by top officials at the FBI. Peter Strzok's manifest

bias trending toward animus casts a pall on this investigation. Bias is so pernicious and malignant as to both taint the process, the result, and the ability to have confidence in either."

By finding that former FBI Director James Comey was "insubordinate" and operating far outside Justice Department rules and prosecutorial ethics in his actions in the Clinton email investigation, IG Horowitz has provided a bulletproof factual refutation of any attempt by Robert Mueller to charge that President Trump obstructed justice when he fired James Comey. The Comey firing, in turn, was the factually thin and constitutionally suspect peg for Mueller's appointment as Special Counsel.

True to form, Mueller is striking back. He has leveled new obstruction of justice charges against former Trump campaign manager Paul Manafort, and on June 15 succeeded in convincing U.S. District Judge Amy Jackson in Washington, D.C. to send Manafort to jail pending trial for alleged witness tampering. The New York Attorney General, who has collaborated with

James Comey, former FBI Director.

Robert Mueller, Special Counsel.

Mueller, filed charges seeking to dissolve the President's charitable foundation, and pressure has increased on Trump's former lawyer, Michael Cohen, to either flip on the President or face Manafort's fate.

This IG report deals only with the Clinton investigation. As of this writing, IG Horowitz continues to investigate improper Justice Department and FBI actions in Russiagate, including the numerous illegal leaks which have fueled the insurrection against Trump. The DOJ and Congress remain locked in a battle over documents concerning MI6's Stefan Halper. If the truth be told about Halper and his British operations against the Trump campaign, further evidence about who actually interfered in the 2016 elections can emerge. It was British intelligence, in the form of a spy ring run by former MI6 head Richard Dearlove, acting on behalf of British geopolitical and strategic interests, in conjunction with the Obama White House and Obama's intelligence directors, not the Russians.

DOJ

Peter Strzok, FBI case officer.

Ohio State University

Lisa Page, FBI lawyer.

The LaRouche Political Action Committee has emphasized that the way to bring the whole affair crashing down, is for the President to declassify everything regarding Russiagate and send it over to the House Intelligence and Judiciary Committees for a full report to the American people, and is circulating a petition to that effect.

What Horowitz Discovered

Horowitz's report, although limited strictly to the Clinton email investigation, reveals a corrupt DOJ and FBI beyond the comprehension of most Americans. Here are the key things the Inspector General found.

FBI case agent Peter Strzok and his mistress, FBI lawyer Lisa Page, exchanged numerous text messages demonstrating overt hostility to Donald Trump, and, in the case of Strzok, the Inspector General found that his overt hostility *could have influenced his investigative actions*. This is a fact which is being uniformly lied about by the news media. As opposed to media portrayals of these lovebirds as just two street FBI agents expressing personal opinions, the Report finds that Strzok vowed to his lover Page that he was going to "stop Trump."

The text exchange, as reported by IG Horowitz, was this:

> **Page:** [Trump's] not ever going to become president, right? Right?!
> **Strzok:** No. No he won't. We'll stop it.

Previously, as the result of the Inspector General's work, texts between Strzok and Page were revealed intimating that they considered that the Russia investigation was an FBI "insurance policy" against Trump. Peter Strzok was the lead case agent on both the Clinton and Russiagate investigations and, with Page, was part of Mueller's initial prosecutorial team. The lead case agent directs all investigative actions in a case. In the body of the IG report, James Comey personally endorses Strzok as one of the few FBI agents capable of conducting a complex counterintelligence investigation such as Russiagate. Page was former FBI Deputy Director Andrew McCabe's special legal counsel, with previous experience in anti-Russian operations. There is a major fight about improper DOJ redaction of other Strzok/Page emails by the DOJ as produced to the House Oversight and Judiciary committees, which will be fueled by these revelations.

Other Highly Biased, Inflammatory Texting

In addition, overtly biased texts about Trump were exchanged by five other FBI employees, including one attorney previously assigned to the Mueller investigation. These texts ridiculed Trump supporters as "poor or middle class" dumb slobs and racist country bumpkins, reflecting the entitled attitude of the Justice Department's professional class which is displayed throughout the IG's report. One of them, the attorney assigned to the Mueller investigation until this year, even declared allegiance to the infamous Trump "resistance." The IG Report recommends that those five agents be referred to the Justice Department's Office of Professional Responsibility for discipline and possibly criminal referral. More about Strzok and Page will most certainly be revealed when the IG releases his report about Russiagate.

FBI Soft Investigative Tactics for Hillary

The initial Clinton email investigation, which began in 2015, was permeated by extraordinarily soft investigative tactics, including consensual interviews rather than compulsory process to obtain evidence, exempting the personal devices of Secretary Clinton's senior aides from examination, unusual immunity and production agreements for Clinton's senior aides, and allowing two attorneys to attend Clinton's witness interview, despite the fact that these attorneys were themselves key witnesses in the probe. The Inspector General's report reveals that the prosecutors in the case were said to be "intimidated" by Clinton's attorneys and worried about retribution should Clinton become President. The decision not to charge Clinton, while supported by prior Department of Justice precedent, is at odds with many other cases involving exposure of classified information.

More significantly, as President Trump has pointed out, the Clinton investigation did not involve targeting lawyers, raiding lawyers' offices, arrests and detentions for purposes of interviews and intimidation, extraordinarily aggressive use of the false statements statutes, no-knock searches, illegal leaks of classified information, classified surveillance, or use of informants and provocateurs for purposes of entrapment—all of which have been employed in the Russiagate investigation against Trump.

In the Clinton affair, the Obama White House publicly declared that Clinton was innocent of any wrongdoing, although no one claimed that somehow Obama was "obstructing" the FBI's investigation with these comments, a claim made each time President Trump speaks. Obama's Attorney General, Loretta Lynch, met with former President Bill Clinton on the tarmac of the Phoenix, Arizona airport in the middle of the Clinton investigation, but did not recuse herself from further participation in the investigation.

Allegedly, the FBI was also presented with a document, still classified, asserting that Russian intelligence had conversations involving Loretta Lynch in which the Attorney General declared her intent to whitewash and exonerate Clinton. In that context, James Comey decided that he alone could provide public credibility for the DOJ decision not to charge Clinton. He conducted an extraordinary press conference on July 5, 2016 in which he announced that Clinton would not be charged with any crime, but that she had been "extraordinarily careless" and negligent with respect to classified information found on her private email server.

According to the IG's report, in the course of this exoneration of Clinton, Comey did not accurately portray essential facts about the Clinton case. Moreover, Comey had begun drafting this statement of exoneration long before Hillary Clinton's interview and long before other essential steps were taken in the case. Comey's press conference violated numerous Justice Department policy and ethical rules governing prosecutorial conduct. He deliberately kept the persons actually legally responsible for making this decision, the Justice Department prosecutors, in the dark about his plans for the press conference.

The IG called Comey's actions a complete contravention of Justice Department rules and declared him "insubordinate." He found that while Comey's actions were not "politically biased," they were based on saving his own skin. Comey was concerned to exonerate his reputation in the Clinton investigation from present and future political criticism. As Alan Dershowitz points out, Comey's motive is far worse in many respects than overt political bias. Comey abused the public trust for purposes of personal gain.

Clinton, Weiner and Huma Abedin

In September 2016, the New York FBI secured the personal laptop of Anthony Weiner, the disgraced sex addict and husband of close Clinton aide Huma Abedin—he had been caught sexting a minor. On his personal computer were tons of Clinton emails, including some marked "Classified." On September 30, 2016, the New York case agent and his supervisor told FBI headquarters about this, but headquarters, including Deputy Director Andrew McCabe and case agent Peter Strzok, sat on the new information. It was only when the New York FBI case agent for Weiner, fearing that he was being set up as a fall guy, pounded repeatedly on the doors of the U.S. Attorney's office in the Southern District of New York (barely escaping being gaslighted as a hopelessly paranoid psychotic by his superiors) that the FBI decided to act in examining the Weiner computer.

Again, Comey decided to take extraordinary action. He alerted the Congress, eleven days before the Presidential election, that the Clinton email investigation was being reopened in order to examine the laptop, resulting in media leaks that Comey knew would occur.

The Inspector General reports that Strzok had decided that the Russiagate investigation against Trump took priority over addressing the new Clinton investigation, and that was the reason for his disinterest in the

Former Democratic Party Congressman Anthony Weiner and his ex-wife Huma Abedin, Vice Chair of Hillary Clinton's 2016 campaign for President.

new Clinton information. This decision was approved by other DOJ officials and, in the context of Strzok's declared jihad against Trump, was, in all probability, permeated by political bias. Again, the Inspector General attributes Comey's actions, in violation of prosecutorial ethics and Justice Department rules, to his personal arrogance and personal reputational concerns, rather than overt bias. Based on the same factual presentation, this writer believes, however, that Comey was acting to create the appearance of being even-handed in the midst of completely illegal and unprecedented actions taken by himself and the FBI with respect to Donald Trump.

The FBI and the News Media

In the course of hinvestigation, the Inspector General found that the FBI was permeated by relationships with the news media far outside specific Justice Department guidelines. As a reward for illegal leaks, FBI agents were showered with tickets to sporting events, dinners, and other gratuities. A chart attached to the main report shows only some of these relationships, involving unnamed reporters and multiple high-level agents of the FBI. The Inspector General is conducting a separate investigation of these leaks. It is noteworthy that Deputy Director Andrew McCabe was

fired as part of this investigation because he lied to the Inspector General about his role in media leaks concerning the Clinton Foundation investigation. McCabe has been referred to the U.S. Attorney for the District of Columbia for possible prosecution.

In the report released yesterday, the Inspector General examined whether McCabe should have recused himself from the Clinton investigation based on his wife Jill McCabe's receipt of hundreds of thousands of dollars for her campaign for Virginia State Senate against incumbent Republican Senator Richard Black. Democrat Jill McCabe's campaign was engineered and funded by the Clintons and former long-time Clinton operative and Virginia Governor Terry McAuliffe. The IG found that McCabe only recused himself after a *Wall Street Journal* article disclosed the Clinton money flowing into Jill McCabe's campaign. McCabe had previously received bad advice from the FBI's ethics office, which had glossed over the obvious conflict. The IG also found that Andrew McCabe ignored the recusal and acted anyway in the investigation.

In addition, the IG found that Assistant Attorney General Peter Kadzik, the former Justice Department liaison with Congress, sought a job for his son with the Clinton campaign while participating in communications and Justice Department discussions about the Clinton investigation. Kadzik should have immediately recused himself. In addition, Kadzik communicated with John Podesta, Clinton's campaign chairman, about internal Justice Department documents concerning an FOIA suit about Clinton's emails.

Overall, and in appropriate context, the Inspector General's report demonstrates completely and conclusively the political and professional bias which permeated FBI and DOJ actions regarding the Clinton email investigation. It also demonstrates, at the same time, that James Comey, the man who has declared himself the arbiter of the nation's morality, acted only in order to salvage his own imagined reputation and persona, while violating numerous professional and ethical norms in the process. More is sure to come when the Inspector General digs into Comey's overtly illegal actions in the Trump investigation.

Invitation to British 'Lawn Jockey' Obama Disgraces the Memory of Mandela

by Ramasimong Phillip Tsokolibane, leader of LaRouche South Africa

June 16—Some people have some screws seriously loose over at the Nelson Mandela Foundation, since they have invited the anti-African former American President Barack Obama to deliver the 16th annual Nelson Mandela lecture on July 17, at the Ellis Park Arena in Johannesburg, in this the hundredth anniversary of the birth of our father. Around 4,000 people are expected to attend this event on the day before Nelson Mandela International Day.

And, as if Obama making this speech were not a sufficient affront, he and his Obama Foundation intend to hold a week-long conference—with

Obama succeeded in dividing his nation, deepening the racial divide, while extending the policies of regime change and war …

workshops and training sessions—of young African "emerging leaders" in Johannesburg, as part of his ongoing recruitment to his cause of serving the neo-colonialists of the British Empire. No doubt he intends to spread chaos in our country and beyond, with the help of former U.S. Ambassador to South Africa Patrick Gaspard—now the president of George Soros' Open Society Foundations—who Obama is bringing with him.

Perhaps some thought it appropriate for Obama to give this lecture, since he was the first black President of the United States. But he was no great leader, and certainly no great President. He was nothing more than a "lawn jockey" for his racist

EIRNS/Joanne McAndrews

LaRouche PAC poster of Obama, on the streets of Washington, D.C., August 2009, commissioned by Lyndon LaRouche.

Ramasimong Phillip Tsokolibane, speaking on "Developing Africa through the BRICS" at a World Land-Bridge conference in Australia, 2015.

masters, who run the British empire. It was their evil interests he served then—and still does—not those of the American people, and especially not the black people, who saw their living conditions decline during his two terms in office. And certainly he did not serve the interests of Africans.

Nelson Mandela successfully brought our nation out of the backwardness and evil of the apartheid system that had actually been inspired by the British Empire, by seeking and securing an alliance with an erstwhile enemy, the Afrikaner and State President F.W. de Klerk. That "impossible" alliance avoided the race war "destiny" desired—and organized for—by the British neo-colonial elite and their assets in our country, and instead provided us the opportunity, as yet not fully realized, to develop not only into Africa's most powerful economy, but also a leader for progress on the world stage.

Obama succeeded in dividing his nation, deepening the racial divide, while extending the policies of regime change and war that had been the hallmark of the prior George W. Bush Presidency. The fake media treats Obama as if he were walking in the tradition of Martin Luther King, Jr., when in fact he is nothing more than an arrogant whore for the City of London and its Wall Street satrapy. He came here in 2013 to arrogantly lecture us that we must not aspire to be a fully developed economy and nation, lest we threaten and destroy nature. He was really spouting the kind of crap typically emitted from the mouths of the British Royals—such as His Royal Virus, Prince Philip, and his Dumbo-like son Charles—about Africans learning to know and enjoy their underdevelopment.

While he was here, I helped to build a demonstration that included hundreds of students, trade unionists, Communists, Muslims, and others to suitably greet Mr. Obama on June 29, 2013 at the University of Johannesburg's Soweto Campus, where he delivered a speech and collected an honorary degree. Members of LaRouche South Africa, the South African branch of the LaRouche movement, at that demonstration, prominently displayed the famous mustachioed Obama poster that accurately depicts him as Adolf Hitler, with which the LaRouche movement had tormented him in the United States.

Nothing has changed about Obama and his essence since that time—except that we have had the happy news that he is out of office, and his chosen successor, Secretary of State Hillary Clinton, was driven from office by the American people. It was a rebellion against the politics of Obama and his female clone Hillary that swept Donald Trump into the White House in the November 2016 election.

So, who would invite this murderous clown, the British "lawn jockey" Obama, to celebrate the life of Nelson Mandela? Only those, whose intention is to defile the memory of Mandela, would give this pro-British, fake American Obama the podium. That's who. *It is still not too late to disinvite Obama*, and that is what I recommend be done. Perhaps we might invite either China's President Xi or Russia's President Putin to deliver the speech instead. This might not be as far-fetched as it might seem to the uninformed; both will be coming to South Africa only a few days after the Mandela lecture, to participate in the BRICS summit, for which our nation is this year's host.

That summit and our involvement in the BRICS embody the true heritage and tradition of our father.

Does anyone have the guts to do what is right? Honor the memory of Nelson Mandela—disinvite Obama!

LAROUCHE'S FOUR POWER CONCEPT

The Miracle of the Singapore Summit

by Michael Billington

June 18—The summit between President Donald Trump and Chairman Kim Jong-un in Singapore on June 12 was certainly one of most important transformational meetings of our time. This event will be recognized in history as confirmation that, as President Trump said in his concluding press conference: "Real change is indeed possible. The past does not have to define the future. Yesterday's conflict does not have to be tomorrow's war. And, as history has proven over and over again, adversaries can become friends. We can honor the sacrifice of our forefathers by replacing the horrors of battle with the blessings of peace. That's what we're doing, and that's what we have done.... Anyone can make war, but only the most courageous can make peace."

President Trump announced after the summit that he had ordered a suspension of U.S.-South Korean military exercises. He told the press that he eventually wants to pull U.S. troops and military bases out of South Korea, but that the exercises, which were both extremely expensive and a serious "provocation" to the North, would be suspended immediately, and remain so as long as the negotiations continue in good faith. This move is in keeping with the standing proposal by both China and Russia for a "double freeze"—the North suspending testing of nuclear weapons and strategic missiles, while the United States and South Korea suspend military exercises.

The old paradigm of imperial division, zero-sum geopolitics, and economic decay is being relegated to the dustbin of history. The new paradigm, now most active in Asia, is extending itself to the entire world through the New Silk Road—a pathway of universal cooperation dedicated to a world of peace and prosperity.

Three Key Meetings in the Unstoppable Silk Road Spirit

Over the weekend of June 9-10, preceding the epoch-changing meeting between President Trump and Chairman Kim Jong-un on June12, three other meetings occurred that reinforce and build on the dramatic change in the course of history for the better, in a manner which cannot be reversed.

White House/Shealah Craighead

Chairman Kim (left) and President Trump signing the Joint Statement at the Singapore Summit, June 12, 2018.

From left to right: Italian Prime Minister Conte, U.S. President Trump, President of the European Commission Juncker, and President of the European Council Tusk at the G-7 Summit in La Malbaie, Canada, June 8, 2018.

The G-7 meeting in Quebec, on June 8-9, shattered the alliance of the once all-powerful leaders of the so-called "free world." President Trump made clear that the institution was impotent without Putin at the table and received support from the new Italian Prime Minister Giuseppe Conte, and implicitly from Japan's Prime Minister Shinzo Abe. The U.S. President left the fractured G-7 event before it ended, skipping the climate change panel.

The Shanghai Cooperation Organization (SCO) summit on June 9-10 in Qingdao, Shandong Province, China represented nearly half the world's population, including notably both India and Pakistan. President Xi Jinping opened the SCO summit by quoting Confucius, who came from Shandong Province: "What a joy to have friends coming from afar"—beautifully capturing the Confucian nature of the win-win approach underlying the Belt and Road Initiative.

On that same weekend of June 9-10, the Schiller Institute sponsored a conference titled, "Dona Nobis Pacem—Grant Us Peace, Through Economic Development," and was concluded by a concert the next day featuring the Schiller Institute Chorus performing Beethoven's Mass in C Major. The conference was keynoted by Schiller Institute founder Helga Zepp-La-Rouche. She was joined by a high-level panel of speakers from Russia, China and the United States. Those speeches were published in full in the June 15 *EIR*. The intent of the conference, as stated by moderator Dennis Speed, was "expressed in the concert poster featuring Martin Luther King, Jr., Robert Kennedy, and Ludwig van Beethoven. Choosing creativity as opposed to tragedy has been the hallmark of the Schiller Institute."

The Korean Miracle and Asian Unity

For the past 68 years, a state of permanent confrontation on the Korean peninsula has not only divided the Korean people, but also has provided the architects of the Cold War in London and Washington with a "cockpit" for war between the West and China and Russia. All nations were instructed by the imperial forces to line up on one side or the other—as John Foster Dulles was fond of saying, "You are either with us or against us." President Barack Obama launched his Pivot to Asia, moving much of the U.S. nuclear strategic forces to Asia, in a ring around China and the Russian Far East, lying all the time that this was necessary to contain North Korea.

Step back and look, through your mind's eye, at the map of Asia. For the very first time in all of history, the entirety of Asia is united behind a unitary concept of peace through development—Russia, China, North and South Korea, Mongolia, Japan, India, Pakistan, Afghanistan, and all of Central Asia and Southeast Asia. The breakthrough in Korea demonstrated an initiative of extraordinary courage by Trump and Kim, but it was only possible because all of Asia, every country without exception, was in accord.

It was, and is, recognized across Asia that ending the Korean division opens up a vast expansion of the New Silk Road process—already begun in Southeast Asia, Central Asia, and South Asia—into East Asia, and Russia's Far East. Both Japan and South Korea, in particular, have the technological capacity needed to bring development to the vast, underpopulated, and resource-rich regions of the Russian Far East and the Arctic, and both nations see their future in terms of cooperation across Eurasia. In addition, the highly skilled work force in North Korea, combined with Russian, Japanese and South Korean technology, can play a crucial role in developing the new frontier for mankind represented by the Russian Far East and the Arctic.

South Korean President Moon Jae-in, during his April 27 summit with Kim Jong-un at the border town

Xinhua/Blue House

South Korean President Moon Jae-in (left) and North Korean leader Kim Jong-un at the Panmunjom Summit, North Korea, May 26, 2018.

CC

Ro Khanna, Democratic Congressman from California.

CC/Korby

Gilad Erdan, Member of the Israeli Knesset.

of Panmunjom, presented Kim with a thumb drive containing a series of development project plans that could be implemented in North Korea, and through North Korea into China and Russia, virtually immediately, if denuclearization and security guarantees for the North could be achieved. President Trump, in his meeting with Kim, showed a ten-minute video posing similar developments which were possible in the North with the success of the negotiations, including pictures of China's High-Speed Rail.

Trump and the Four Powers

While the war mongers in Europe and the United States howl about President Trump "coddling dictators" and "capitulating" to Kim Jong-un's demand to end the military exercises, their evil intentions are recognized by a rapidly expanding majority of the citizens of the United States. A group of 15 Democrats in the House of Representatives, led by California Congressman Ro Khanna, are now supporting Trump's initiative with North Korea, and have attacked the leaders of the Democratic Party for sounding like the neoconservatives in the Republican Party. Some have (accurately) accused the likes of Chuck Schumer and Nancy Pelosi of preferring nuclear war, rather than supporting the President on anything.

There are other "cockpits" for war in the world, such as the India-Pakistan conflict, and the Middle East imbroglio—both created by the British with the intention that such seemingly intractable conflicts and per-

manent warfare would provide the necessary "divide and conquer" context for the lords of the global financial system to maintain power over the world.

Now, a solution for the India-Pakistan conflict is within reach, through cooperation in the Shanghai Cooperation Organization (SCO). And, following the Singapore summit, Israel's Public Security Minister Gilad Erdan (the number two lawmaker on the Likud party's Knesset list) called the event "a tremendous achievement." Asked if Trump should hold a similar summit with Iran's President Hassan Rouhani, Erdan responded: "Given Trump's values, both as expressed during the election and afterwards in his actions, it would not be terrible if such a meeting happens." Indeed, both Russia and China would be most willing to facilitate such a meeting, which could result in discussions aimed at resolving the entire regional crisis, starting with the withdrawal of all foreign forces from Syria. This will clearly be on the agenda of the expected summit between Trump and Putin in July.

President Trump's cooperation with the Asian nations to bring about this transformation provides a model for resolving the other crises around the world. Lyndon LaRouche has long insisted that the root of depression and war in the world today lies in the looming bankruptcy of the world monetary system centered in the City of London and Wall Street, and that the only means of ending that danger is the coming together of the four great powers and cultures in the world—Russia, China, India and the United States—as we see it coming into being today.

Speaking on Oct. 10, 2009 at the Seventh Annual Session of the World Public Forum—Dialogue of Civilizations on the Island of Rhodes in Greece, LaRouche said that he had forecast the financial crisis of 2008, but that the failure of the Bush and Obama administrations to implement the banking reforms he had proposed, based on Glass-Steagall restoration, meant that "it is no longer possible to do what I proposed then, back in 2007." The crisis had become global, threatening a breakdown of the entire world financial structure. He continued:

> Therefore, the task, as I defined it, is, if Russia, and the United States, and China, and India, agree, as a group of countries, to initiate and force a reorganization of the world financial and credit system, under those conditions, with long-term agreements, of the same type that Franklin Roosevelt had uttered before his death, in 1944, under key nations, the intention of Roosevelt all these years later, could have been realized, and we could do that, today. That's our chance: Either we do that, or we go under. Can we have the United States, under an improved Presidency—and it does require improvement—can we have the United States, Russia, China, and India, become a bloc of countries, which each have different characteristics, but if they recognize among themselves, that they have a common interest, they will adapt to each other, and respect each other's different characteristics. The result of this, will be the elimination of the monetary system of the world that has been dominating European civilization since the Peloponnesian War.

> The imperial systems of the world, are not the United Kingdom, for example, but the British *system* is an imperial system. It's an imperial system because of its role in an international monetary system. We no longer have nations which control their own money: We have an international monetary system that does control their money. If you control the monetary market, the monetary system, you control the world.

EIRNS/Stefan Tolksdorff
Lyndon LaRouche presents his Four Powers proposal at the World Public Forum—Dialogue of Civilizations (Rhodes Forum) in Rhodes, Greece, October 9, 2009.

> The monetary system is now a disease. We have to put the power over monetary systems, back in the hands of sovereign governments.

The "four power" agreement LaRouche spoke of back in 2009 has now been placed squarely on the agenda of world history in the making, through the breakthrough in Korea, resolving a problem that many considered unresolvable. Whether or not the United States extends its cooperation to fully embrace the New Silk Road, and bring this cooperation to bear in an overall reform of the western financial system, as laid out in LaRouche's Four Laws, will depend on the actions taken by the citizens of the western nations to drive this process forward.

Helga Zepp-LaRouche has taken the first step in mobilizing such actions, as presented in this issue of *EIR*. In her article, "EU Summit Must Follow Singapore Example! History Is Now Written in Asia!" Zepp-LaRouche poses that the extreme crisis in Europe, driven by economic decay and the drastic refugee situation created by the perpetual war policy in Southwest Asia, could and must be resolved by transforming the upcoming EU summit into a forum on the development of Africa and Southwest Asia, inviting Chinese and African leaders to attend. She concludes:

> The crisis in Europe, the migrant crisis, the crisis of the German government—have all assumed such dimensions, that the opportunity for a change in direction of policy absolutely has arrived. Needed now, are the people to make the change.

As President Trump said after the summit: "It's a very great moment in the history of the world." Or, recasting Benjamin Franklin's famous comment, upon successfully establishing a "more perfect union" for Americans in the 1787 Constitution: "It's a New Paradigm, if you can keep it."

Sino-India Relations Must Be Reset In Wake of Rapid Changes in Eurasia

by Ramtanu Maitra

June 16—Last April, Indian Prime Minister Narendra Modi flew to Wuhan, China to have a two-day, informal one-on-one summit with Chinese President Xi Jinping, April 27-28. The objective of the two leaders was to repair and re-energize stuttering Sino-India relations. Following that informal summit—although much of the content of their deliberation remains confidential—they issued a joint statement indicating their agreement to push the reset button. Meanwhile, there are signs that a broader cooperative participation in support of Afghanistan was mooted, and they agreed to speed up economic cooperation under the Bangladesh-China-India-Myanmar (BCIM) framework.

Manoj Joshi, an Indian journalist, in analyzing the outcome of the informal summit, wrote:

PIB India

Indian Prime Minister Narendra Modi (left) and Chinese President Xi Jinping at their summit in Wuhan, China, April 27-28, 2018.

An important outcome is their decision to provide 'strategic guidance' to their respective militaries to keep peace along the Sino-Indian border. This would involve enhanced official level meetings to build trust and understanding, and implementation of existing confidence building agreements and institutional mechanisms to resolve problems in the border areas.

Additionally, it was noted that the two sides also recognize the common threat posed by terrorism and the need to oppose it in all its forms and manifestations. India and China have decided to cooperate in joint projects in Afghanistan and we could also see possible collaboration in third countries such as Nepal or Bangladesh. ("The Wuhan Summit," *Observer Research Foundation*, May 1, 2018)

The Wuhan Effect

Reflecting on the Wuhan summit and pointing out that it was the 13th summit between the two—they met again at the summit of the Shanghai Cooperation Organization (SCO) in Qingdao, China on June 9-10—China's Ambassador to India, Luo Zhaohui, wrote, in an article in the Indian daily, *The Tribune:*

The two leaders further deepened their understanding with each other and shared similar views on the historical position, stage and goal of development of China and India. The two sides viewed each other's developmental intentions in a positive way and decided to build a Closer Developmental Partnership in an equal, mutually beneficial and sustainable manner.

Prime Minister Modi briefed President Xi on India's "neighborhood first" policy and the concept of "the world as one," which are quite similar with President Xi's idea of "neighborhood diplomacy as high priority," and "to build a community of shared future for mankind," Ambassador wrote. ("My Interpretation of Wuhan Summit," *The Tribune*, May 6, 2018)

Less than forty days later, Modi and Xi met again, this time at Qingdao, China during the two-day (June 9-10) SCO summit, attended by the heads of state or government of the Central Asian countries, China, Russia, India and six observer states. Less than two weeks before Qingdao, on June 1, Modi delivered the keynote speech at the Shangri-La Dialogue in Singapore, addressing an issue that will surely have a positive effect in Sino-India relations.

In recent months, anti-China geopoliticians, mostly from West, have been urging India to become part of an Indo-Pacific alliance, ostensibly to "counter China's geopolitical ambitions." In addition, efforts were made to label the annual Malabar naval exercise—which has been conducted for years between the United States, Japan and India—as a Quadrilateral Security Dialogue, by bringing in Australia to counter China's growing naval strength. The anti-China mob wants to merge that naval exercise with the Indo-Pacific alliance, thus forming a well-defined axis against China that would include two non-Asian nations.

But at the Shangri-La Dialogue, Modi avoided using the word "Quad" (Quadrilateral Security Dialogue consisting of the United States, India, Japan and Australia, and conceived by some as a counterbalance to China's rising presence in the Indo-Pacific), by separating the Indo-Pacific alliance from the security dialogue. At least a month before Modi's Shangri-La speech, India had turned down Australia's request to participate in the now ongoing Malabar Exercise—a major setback for the proponents of a Quadrilateral Security Dialogue.

At Singapore, Modi pushed aside misconceptions that India wants the Indo-Pacific to be an exclusive

U.S. Navy/William McCann

Malabar 2018 war games exercise, June 12, 2018.

club, saying: "… India does not see the Indo-Pacific Region as a strategy or as a club of limited members. Nor as a grouping that seeks to dominate." He also said,

> India's own engagement in the Indo-Pacific Region—from the shores of Africa to that of the Americas—will be inclusive…. That is the foundation of our civilizational ethos—of pluralism, co-existence, openness and dialogue. The ideals of democracy that define us as a nation also shape the way we engage the world.

Modi did not comment on America's renaming of the U.S. Pacific Command as the Indo-Pacific Command a few days earlier. Instead, he lauded India's "multi-layer relations with China," saying: "Strong and stable relations between our two nations are an important factor for global peace and progress." His remarks were almost immediately echoed by the Chinese delegation attending the Shangri-La Dialogue.

Modi's remarks that India does not see the Indo-Pacific Region as directed against any country, dooms the Quad.

On the other hand, the issues dividing the neighboring nations, India and China—the two most populous in the world, occupying a large part of the Asian landmass—are complex and are not expected to be resolved any time soon. However, the Wuhan summit, and the subsequent interactions, suggest that both leaders are keen to bypass those major issues—while not abandoning efforts to resolve them—and not consider them to be insurmountable walls. Instead, they chose to jointly participate in enhancing bilateral economic interactions, while cooperating in the security and development of infrastructure of the Eurasian region. This choice brings into play the BRICS association, the Belt and Road Initiative (BRI), the BCIM framework, the China-Pakistan Economic Corridor (CPEC), and the SCO, as we shall see.

But first, the troublesome background.

The Doklam Stand-Off

One of the main reasons for the reset was the necessity to ensure that bilateral relations do not suffer further damage as a result of two major, unresolved issues. After all, China and India are the fastest-growing large nations, each with more than 1.2 billion people, many of whom are poor; growing cooperation between the two is essential for the future.

One of these unresolved issues is the Doklam border confrontation. In June 2017, Chinese troops began construction to extend a road south into Doklam, in an area claimed by both China and Bhutan, an ally of India (see map). The Doklam plateau—at the tri-junction of India, China, and Bhutan—is an uninhabited area used mostly for seasonal cattle grazing. Two days later, Indian troops entered Doklam to stop the Chinese project. Jingoistic campaigns by media managers in both countries followed, and went to great lengths to prove who was right and who was wrong.

India and China announced on August 28 that they had agreed to remove their troops from the site at which the confrontation had occurred. After this agreement—reached just days before the ninth BRICS summit was to begin on September 4 in Xiamen, China—there was an urgency to put the relationship back on the right track, even while both sides remained vigilant in Doklam.

The conflict is complex. The Modi administration is in the process of making the economic development of this area a priority, to enhance a robust economic pres-

PIB India

Chinese State Councilor Yang Jiechi (left) meeting with Indian Prime Minister Narendra Modi to resolve the border dispute in Doklam. New Delhi, December 22, 2017.

Wikimedia Commons/Nilesh Shukla

The disputed Doklam area is identified here by its Tibetan name, "Donglang region."

ence in Southeast Asia. More concretely, and of equal importance, Doklam is less than 100 miles from the strategic Siliguri Corridor, sometimes called the Chicken Neck, which connects India's main body to its eight northeastern states. The corridor, varying from 13 to 25 miles wide, is India's only road link to its relatively unstable and underdeveloped northeastern states. These states, spread over 105,000 square miles, have a combined population of 46 million. This eight-state area borders China in the north, Myanmar in the east, Bangladesh in the southwest, Nepal in the west, and Bhutan in the northwest.

While the Doklam stand-off is not a dispute over the Sino-Indian border itself, there is a border dispute between the two countries. It is extensive, and it is a long way from being settled. On Dec. 22, 2017, India and China held the 20th round of talks on the decades-old border dispute. These talks were not designed to tackle the disputed borders head-on, but merely to establish peace and tranquility along the Line of Actual Control (LAC). However, even the LAC has not been fully defined yet. What is encouraging, however, is that the 20th round of talks did not confine itself to the same old border issues, but reportedly covered the wide gamut of nettling issues between the two governments.

As of now, both sides recognize that before the border disputes can be adequately addressed with the specific intent to demarcate the border and identify it as an international border, other measures must be taken to prevent flash-points from suddenly cropping up in these distant and desolate places, embittering bilateral relations. One of India's leading academics on Sino-Indian relations, Mohan Guruswamy, wrote in December 2017,

> Both countries agree that these are legacies of history and cannot be solved in the short or medium term and are best left for the future. But what causes friction between the two is that they do not have agreed a Line of Actual Control (LAC) to separate the jurisdictions under the control of their armies. The perceptions of the LAC differ at many places. In some places it might be by just a few meters, and elsewhere by tens of kilometers. ("Why India and China's Border Disputes Are So Difficult to Resolve," *South China Morning Post*, December 17, 2017).

What Guruswamy wrote is now very much in focus for both Beijing and New Delhi.

Trouble Over the CPEC, and BRI

Another major area of difficulty between India and China stems from the construction of the China-Pakistan Economic Corridor (CPEC), a part of China's Belt and Road Initiative (BRI). The CPEC extends from China's Xinjiang province to the Arabian Sea, traversing Pakistan from its northern border to its shore in the south. India has spurned China's invitation to participate in this project. It became evident when the leaders of 29 countries and representatives from more than 130 nations gathered in Beijing in May 2017 for the Belt and Road Forum. India declined the invitation, having decided not to participate in the deliberations.

Officially, India's Modi government says that India cannot join the BRI. A major part of the BRI in India's neighborhood is the CPEC, it says, which enters Pakistan through the northwestern Gilgit-Baltistan area of Jammu and Kashmir, a disputed territory that New Delhi claims, but which has remained under Pakistan's occupation since 1948. India's Foreign Ministry spokesman, Gopal Baglay, told the media that "no country can accept a project that ignores its core con-cerns on sovereignty and territorial integrity." ("One Belt One Road: China-Pakistan Warmth, India Skips Summit," *The Indian Express,* May 14, 2017)

But India went beyond this to speak of the conduct of connectivity initiatives in general, as a reason for not attending the Belt and Road Forum. "We are of firm belief that connectivity initiatives must be based on universally recognized international norms, good governance, rule of law, openness, transparency and equality," India's Foreign Ministry spokesman said, adding that "we have been urging China to engage in a meaningful dialogue" on the BRI. ("Official Spokesperson's Response to a Query on Participation of India in OBOR/BRI Forum," Ministry of External Affairs, Government of India, May 13, 2017) The just concluded Wuhan summit appears to be at least a step in the right direction.

China continues to urge India to join the BRI. China acknowledged India's objection with respect to the CPEC. On Nov. 17, 2017, speaking at the Centre for Chinese and South-East Asian Studies in the School of Language at Jawaharlal Nehru University in New Delhi, China's Ambassador to India, Luo Zhaohui, said that China may consider alternative routes through Jammu and Kashmir to address India's concerns regarding the CPEC, which passes through Pakistan-administered Kashmir. "We can change the name of CPEC. Create an alternative corridor through Jammu and Kashmir, Nathu La pass or Nepal to deal with India's concerns," he said on that occasion. ("China proposes alternative routes for CPEC via J&K, Nepal," *The Hindu*, Kallol Bhattacherjee: Nov. 18, 2017). So far, nothing further has been heard about such an alternative route.

In addition to these two major obstacles to improvement of Sino-Indian relations, as one could expect, there are many other disagreements between the two countries. Seemingly, the maturing of their relations, and the exigency to achieve it, has put these niggling issues presently on the back burner, as they move forward to work together on more important issues.

With that as the background of relations between the two countries, conventional wisdom says a rapid improvement of relations between India and China is unlikely. However, conventional wisdom has its limitations grounded in time and space. Global political situations, particularly in the Eurasian region, have changed, and these changes are well reflected in the intent of both China and India to participate in that process. In other words, a new space for broader cooperation has emerged over a period of time.

Chinese President Xi Jinping (left) and Indian Prime Minister Narendra Modi at the Shanghai Cooperation Organization summit in Qingdao, China, June 9, 2018.

The rise of China and India as major economic powers and their close relations with Russia adjoining Europe could make the Eurasian zone, along with Southeast and East Asia, a motor for development in the coming decades. Both India and China have done very well in maintaining, and even upgrading, their relations with these two areas of future prosperity.

In describing these changes, topmost on the list should be the growing prowess of Russia, India and China within the five-country BRICS organization—Brazil, Russia, India, China, and South Africa. Although the domestic problems within South Africa and Brazil have somewhat stymied the BRICS' expected growth as a powerful global grouping of nations, it has not curbed the growth of the other three, nor has it slowed down their economic and political interactions—a key ingredient for future developments.

India and Pakistan Join SCO

In addition to BRICS, the interaction between Russia, India, and China has been given a boost by their becoming the three most important nations in laying out the policies of the less well-known Shanghai Cooperation Organization (SCO). "The SCO member states account for one-fourth of the world's GDP, 43 percent of the world's population and 23 percent of the global territory," Russian President Putin told the China Media Group, which includes the CGTN English channel. He stressed the "rapid economic growth of China, India and Russia, all of which are major players in the organi-

zation." ("Putin Names India, China and Russia as 'Major Players' in SCO," *The Hindustan Times*," June 6, 2018)

The SCO was originally formed in 1996 as the Shanghai Five—China, Russia, Kazakhstan, Kyrgyzstan, and Tajikistan. Following the inclusion of Uzbekistan as a full member in 2001, it was re-founded in Shanghai that year and renamed the SCO. In 2017, India and Pakistan became full members. SCO also has six dialogue partners, including Afghanistan.

SCO was originally set up as a confidence-building forum to demilitarize borders. However, the organization's goals and agenda have since broadened to include increased military and counter-terrorism cooperation and intelligence sharing. The SCO has also intensified its focus on regional economic initiatives such as the recently announced integration of the China-led BRI and the Russia-led Eurasian Economic Union.

The potential for the SCO to be effective is manifold. Beside the fact that the leadership of the organization rests in the hands of the "Big Three"—China, Russia and India—the organization has provided another platform for the heads of state of Russia, India and China to interact directly and deal with the acute regional security situation. By including Pakistan as a full member, and having Afghanistan as an observer, an environment has thus been created in which terrorism and drug-trafficking can be addressed. These two destructive forces, if not dealt with firmly and with steady hands, could disrupt the development plans of the "Big Three," weakening their ability to play an effective and positive global role.

A Task Cut Out for SCO

Terrorism already affects India, Russia, China and the five Central Asian "stan" countries—Kazakhstan, Uzbekistan, Turkmenistan, Kyrgyzstan and Tajikistan. Terrorism in the Indian part of Jammu and Kashmir, instigated from outside, continues despite various measures undertaken by New Delhi in recent years. Heroin/opium moving out of Afghanistan through Central Asia and Pakistan has bolstered financing of terrorists throughout the region. In India's northeast, where many small but violent secessionist groups operate, heroin and synthetic drugs come in from its east. New Delhi is concerned about these developments and would like to shut down the conduit.

In Russia, particularly in the northern Caucasus, Islamic jihadis have exhibited their presence over the decades. Among the most affected areas are Chechnya,

Terrorist video message from the militant Jihadist organization, Caucasus Emirate, 2015.

Dagestan, Ingushetia and North Ossetia, but also Tatarstan. Maintaining stability and enhancing prosperity in these areas are important for Russia, since Russia shares borders with the "stan" countries of Central Asia. All Muslim states that were for decades part of the Soviet Union, are now independent nations and are full members of the SCO, where Russia is a major force to reckon with.

For China, besides facing difficulties in dealing with militant Uyghur secessionists in Xinjiang province, a terrorist-free Eurasian zone is an essential requirement to make its BRI viable and beneficial for the host and recipient countries. BRI highways and railroads run through "stan" countries to Russia and Europe, and also through Iran to Gulf countries. China has invested heavily in this enterprise in order to make these transport corridors a success. However, if China does not step up to the plate in dealing with the drug traffickers and terrorists who roam virtually with abandon in these sparsely populated areas, Beijing's dream of interlinking China through roads and railways with Central Asia, Europe and Middle East could end up as rubble.

The BRI is not a one-shot deal. Its utility will be realized on the basis of its 24/7 operations spread over years to come. That means the entire area around these installations has to remain terrorist-free; it is a task China must undertake in conjunction with the SCO and in its bilateral relations with the countries involved. Moreover, India-China relations, when allowed to develop fully, have an enormous potential in accomplishing this difficult task.

From Wuhan, a Ray of Hope for Afghanistan

At the Wuhan summit, Modi and Xi agreed to participate in joint infrastructure-related projects in Afghanistan. Although no specific projects have been spelled out yet, it is likely that these will be designed to bring some relief to the war-ravaged Afghans. "There will be more China-India projects in the region in the pipeline, some of which will involve a third party," Vice Foreign Minister Kong Xuanyou told a media briefing at the end of the Wuhan summit. "The decision will have a bearing on the region and on Afghanistan's role as a 'roundabout' of cooperation in Asia," said Barnett Rubin, Senior Fellow at the Center on International Cooperation and former advisor to the UN Mission to Afghanistan (UNAMA).

Rubin continues,

The message to Pakistan is clear: China welcomes India's legitimate role in Afghanistan. For years the Pakistan military has rationalized its support for the Taliban and other pressures on Kabul by citing the threat posed by the Indian presence in Afghanistan. Now without saying a word directly to Pakistan, China has announced that it not only recognizes but wants to cooperate with the Indian presence in Afghanistan. ("Sino-Indian Project in Afghanistan Signals Cooperation, Message to Pakistan," Sutirtho Patranobis, *The Hindustan Times*, May 1, 2018)

India had long been involved in Afghanistan, building, schools, hospitals, roads and even hydropower stations. However, none of that has done much to lower the level of seemingly unending hostilities, emanating partly

The Afghan-India Friendship Dam in western Afghanistan.

China-Pakistan Economic Corridor (CPEC) into Afghanistan, according to a report prepared by the non-profit Boao Forum for Asia (BFA). The BFA, formed by China in 2001 on the sidelines of the World Economic Forum in Davos, Switzerland, has held an annual conference since 2001 in Boao, a city in China's Hainan Province. The report, according to Xinhua news agency, says that—

> China-Pakistan Economic Corridor (CPEC), a flagship project under the Belt and Road Initiative, has not only improved local infrastructure but also is extending toward Afghanistan, reducing poverty, the hotbed of terrorism,

WAPCOS

and bringing better prospects for local people's lives. ("China Taking Pak Economic Corridor All the Way to Afghanistan: Report," NDTV, April 9, 2018)

The Chinese initiative has shone a glimmer of hope. Pakistan's Chief of Army Staff, Gen. Qamar Javid Bajwa, led a delegation that met with Afghan President Ashraf Ghani in Kabul. "They discussed implementation of the Afghanistan-Pakistan Action Plan for Peace, the fight against terrorism, reducing violence, and the Afghan-owned peace process," Ghani's deputy spokesman Shahussain Murtazawi said, according to TOLO news of Afghanistan. "Effective and important talks with Pakistan help us to find logical solutions for historical and fundamental problems," Murtazawi said on June 13.

According to the Kabul government, the difference between the June 12 meeting and previous meetings was that the two sides agreed not to repeat "mistaken" politics, TOLO news reported. "Mr. Bajwa clearly said that the continuance of mistaken politics is neither in Afghanistan nor in Pakistan's favor and politics should change in line with cases," said Omid Maisam, deputy spokesman for Afghanistan's Chief Executive Abdullah Abdullah.

BCIM, the Other Topic at Wuhan

At Wuhan, the joint statement said that China and India would speed up the Bangladesh-China-India-

---

because of a large presence of U.S. troops in the country. One other problem that ensures hostilities, and discussed widely, is Pakistan's unwillingness to cooperate in interdicting the movement of terrorists from Pakistan to Afghanistan and vice-versa. For years, Pakistan has denied this shortcoming. But a sign of change has shown up recently, and the credit surely belongs to China:

> On December 16, [2017] Beijing hosted the first China-Afghanistan-Pakistan Foreign Ministers' Dialogue. The three countries' foreign ministers—China's Wang Yi, Afghanistan's Salahuddin Rabbani and Pakistan's Khawaja Muhammad Asif—attended. The three countries agreed to establish a trilateral dialogue mechanism in June aimed at reinforcing trilateral cooperation in politics, economics and security. Afghanistan will host the second dialogue in Kabul in 2018.
>
> During the press conference after the meeting, Wang announced that "Afghanistan and Pakistan agreed to improve bilateral relations as soon as possible and to realize harmonious co-existence, promising to resolve their concerns through comprehensive dialogue and consultation." ("Why Is China Holding the China-Pakistan-Afghanistan Dialogue Now?" Charlotte Gao, *The Diplomat*, Dec. 27, 2017)

Stability and peace in Afghanistan is of particular importance to China. China has plans to extend the

Myanmar (BCIM) Corridor project. Chinese Vice-Foreign Minister Kong Xuanyou, briefing newsmen in Beijing on April 28 about the summit outcome—and playing down India-China differences over the BRI—said:

> … When it comes to connectivity our impression is that China and India do not have a principled disagreement. Actually the two countries are working on the BCIM which is an important part of BRI and for the BCIM corridor, India does not oppose it. Actually, it is an important partner in this cooperation. At the same time BCIM is progressing very smoothly. ("Wuhan Summit: India, China To Step Up Policy Coordination," *Press Trust of India*, April 30, 2018)

However, on the ground, BCIM is not progressing very smoothly. That is the reason that Modi and Xi brought it up in their discussions—to give it a push. The BCIM Economic Corridor idea emerged in the 1990s for possible cooperation involving southwestern China, eastern India, and the whole of Myanmar and Bangladesh. Conceived as a sub-regional economic cooperation project, the BCIM initiative was launched in 1999 in Kunming, the capital of China's Yunnan province. Two prominent objectives have driven the BCIM initiative—one is economic integration of the sub-region that would also enable integration of Asia; the other is development of the border regions. ("The BCIM Economic Corridor: Prospects and Challenges," K. Yhome, Observer Research Foundation, Feb. 10, 2017) The India-China Joint Statement of May 2013 endorsed the BCIM officially at the highest level.

Perhaps one of the reasons that the BCIM did not take off is that it has remained within the realm of the sub-regional developmental plans. Both India and China have grown significantly since China launched the BRI, and the Modi administration has been keen to develop northeastern states for a strong presence in Southeast Asia. The Wuhan summit declaration makes it clear that the time has come for the BCIM to take off.

Writing in the Bangladesh weekly *The Star* in 2014, Prof. Mustafizur Rahman of Bangladesh pointed out that—

> the idea driving the proposed BCIM initiative was that, by drawing on [their] respective comparative advantages, all the four BCIM countries could expect to make significant gains through operationalization of the economic corridor, sub-regional cooperation within the BCIM, and BCIM-wide economic cooperation. These gains are envisaged to accrue from greater market access for goods, services and energy, elimination of non-tariff barriers, better trade facilitation, investment in infrastructure development, joint exploration and development of mineral, water, and other natural resources, development of value and supply chains based on comparative advantages, by translating comparative advantages into competitive advantages, and through closer people to people contact. ("BCIM—Economic Corridor: An Emerging Opportunity," *The Star*, March 15, 2014)

And If the Korean Crisis Ends?

Finally, a further opportunity for improving India-China relations is emerging in the eastern end of the Eurasian zone. The crisis of the Korean peninsula has been hanging fire for more than six decades. Located close to three major nations—Japan, China and Russia—the Korean peninsula had long been teetering close to war. The open hostility between the two Korean states, following the four years of war (1950-53) and division of the country along the 38th Parallel, kept the area on the brink of a war throughout the Cold War. Although the Cold War ended in 1991, the situation on the Korean peninsula remained frozen in the past.

Only recently have both sides shown an eagerness to change. In a historic summit at Singapore on June 12, U.S. President Donald Trump met with North Korea's Chairman, Kim Jung-un, and together they laid a foundation for achieving peace on the peninsula. It is acknowledged that if and when this peace is achieved, it will provide a tremendous boost to the entire region. The process of industrialization and economic development of North Korea will bring the major powers in the region closer. It will also help secure the region.

It is evident that the establishment of peace and stability in the Korean peninsula could step up cooperation between India and China; both maintain full diplomatic relations with North Korea. And furthering of cooperation between these two nations will ensure growth and stability in Asia, the home of about 4.5 billion people, as well as the world beyond.

Trump and His Eurasian Allies Outflank the Dying British Empire

This is the edited transcript of the June 14, 2018 Schiller Institute New Paradigm webcast, an interview with the founder of the Schiller Institutes, Helga Zepp-LaRouche. She was interviewed by Harley Schlanger. A video of the webcast is available.

Harley Schlanger: Hello. I'm Harley Schlanger with the Schiller Institute. Welcome to this week's webcast with our founder, Helga Zepp-LaRouche.

At the end of last year, at the end of 2017, Helga forecast that 2018 would be the year in which the era of geopolitics would end. I think the developments of the last week have been a major step toward that actually coming to fruition, with the extraordinary summit in Singapore between President Trump and Kim Jong-un of North Korea, as well as the Shanghai Cooperation Organization summit in China, and then, with the collapse of the old order, the meeting of the G-7—or G-6, or G-whatever—in Canada.

Helga, why don't we start with the developments that took place in Singapore? This was an earth-shaking event and worthy of being the first topic of our discussion today.

Helga Zepp-LaRouche: I'm actually quite pleased to tell you, and you may know about it, two Norwegian parliamentarians have nominated President Trump for the 2019 Nobel Peace Prize. Now, I find this very appropriate, in contrast to the Nobel Peace Prize being given to Obama for absolutely nothing, just the contrary. I think this development of North Korea and the United States finding a way to completely transform an old adversarial relationship into one of cooperation and a bright future, is really a fantastic development. I know that all the mainstream media of the West are having apoplectic attacks over this, but if you look at it, I think it is absolutely promising.

First of all, the facts you all know: Trump and Kim agreed on the complete denuclearization of North

White House/Shealah Craighead

President Donald Trump and Chairman Kim Jong-un at the Singapore Summit.

Korea, in return for the prospect of making North Korea a prosperous and wealthy country.

I find it very interesting that the White House, between Trump and the National Security Council, produced a four-minute video, in Korean and English, portraying the two options for North Korea: One being the old status and war, and the other a complete modernization of the country, with modern railways. The video,—even shows the Chinese maglev running, and people prosperous and productive. I think this was very good, because this video is exactly what will happen, and it goes very far beyond a similar video which was produced by South Korea in the past. Trump showed it to Kim Jong-un in the meetings, and then he also showed it before giving his press conference.

I watched his entire press conference, and I must say, I would advise all of you, our viewers, to do likewise. Because you hear so much about Trump being this and that, and the way he conducted himself in this lengthy press conference, fencing off the most typical, old-fashioned thinking, questions from mainly American journalists—he did not let himself be provoked. Journalists pestered him with, "What will you do, what is your punishment if North Korea does not comply?" But he wouldn't go into this trap; he just said he was very confident that the process was on a good way.

Very important also was his announcement that the United States would stop what he called "war games," the U.S.-South Korea military maneuvers. This is obviously very important psychologically for the North Koreans, because having war games on your door step all the time creates permanent psychological terror.

Trump: We Are Captains of Our Fate

People who are still forming their judgment about how to look at this, should consider that the South Korean people are absolutely enthusiastic. They were happy in the streets. South Korean President Moon Jae-in, who watched the live stream coming from the conference in Singapore, applauded several times. The unification of Germany took place now almost 29 years ago. Many Germans may still remember the absolute jubilance and happiness of families hugging each other, who hadn't been together for very many years; friends falling into each other's arms, and kissing each other. And it was a joy!

That the German unification did not produce only happiness afterwards had to do with the larger geostrategic environment. Bush, and Thatcher and Mitterrand all were extremely hostile to the process of German unification, and therefore the East German states were practically economically dismantled, pretty much. The environment in North Korea is obviously completely different.

I'm very optimistic that the Korean process will succeed, for the very simple reason that this is taking place in a completely different strategic context, namely of the Belt and Road Initiative—the integration of the Belt and Road Initiative with the Eurasian Economic Union, and these kinds of economic development plans, that also Russia spoke about. China has said they would contribute, and together with the United States, take over security guarantees for North Korea. These economic plans take place in the context of the intention to develop the Far East of Russia, to integrate it with all of Asia, which was discussed at the Eastern Economic Forum in Vladivostok last September and in the inter-Korean dialogue in April between the two presidents of the two Koreas.

So I think the perspective is that North Korea, soon, will be integrated into the Eurasian transport system, the two railways will soon connect to the Trans-Siberian Railway and to the Chinese railway system, and that you will have a complete transformation of this part of the world. And I think Trump is absolutely right in what he said, "The past does not have to define our future." Real change is possible. I think this is a very good development, and all the nay-sayers they should just go home and think.

A Philosophical Foundation

Schlanger: The point you just made I think was one of the most important: Both presidents talked about overcoming the past. Kim Jong-un said that we need to develop a new friendly attitude between our peoples, as opposed to the animus. And of course, that's what Trump has displayed in both the lead-up to the summit and in the aftermath of the summit. This is one of the things that is angering the people you mentioned that aren't happy about this—the fact that he's saying, look, this is a new period, it's a new time.

Helga, this probably the most important thing—this idea of entering into a new era. And this is, of course, what you've been talking about for years, and we now are on the verge of a new emergence of a Eurasian Century.

Zepp-LaRouche: Yes. I think that spirit is clearly prevalent in Asia. It was also the expressed view of Chinese Foreign Minister Wang Yi after the SCO summit in Qingdao, China. This summit was an extraordinary milestone, where Wang Yi afterwards said, the SCO represents 3.1 billion people, and it is already now a completely new system of international relations, built on mutual trust, on cooperation, on friendship, on common aims, and it is a new model, that leaves behind and transcends the old geopolitical order, Cold War, exclusive clubs, clash of civilizations—all of these are left behind, and a new era of cooperation has been established.

This was very beautiful, because the summit,— the initial banquet was opened by President Xi Jinping with a reference to Confucius. He said Qingdao is in Shandong province, which is the home of Confucius and Confucianism, and that Confucius should guide the future of the Shanghai Cooperation Organization.

India-China discussion at the SCO meeting.

Xi Jinping is a philosopher. Just contrast that—can you imagine any European leader opening an EU summit with the words, "we should have Plato's spirit, or Shakespeare's spirit, or Schiller's spirit guide the future of the European Union"? Nothing is more impossible to think than that at this moment.

So, I think the future lies in Asia. And the kind of cooperation and determination to create a better world for all people living on this planet is being realized in Asia right now.

And I think it was a very good thing that President Trump is definitely helping the best he can to make this order succeed, despite the trade tensions and despite the remaining problems which are still there. I'm absolutely confident that the spirit and the dynamic of this new phenomenon, these new forces of which Wang Yi spoke—he said there are new forces at work which make this all possible,— and I think that that is the dynamic of our time, the trend of our time. And it's a good thing. It's wonderful, and everybody who loves humanity and who loves peace should be absolutely happy.

Schlanger: I knew it wasn't just the discussions of trade deals or security concerns, that would make you happy, but the fact that the Shanghai Cooperation Organization took place on a philosophical level. And this is spilling over into the talks between President Trump and the North Korean President, for precisely the reason that the other countries are involved in the Korean summit. Trump made a point to thank China, Japan, South Korea, and Russia.

Helga, I think there may be a couple more things you want to bring up on the Shanghai Cooperation Organization meeting. India and Pakistan participated—this really has become something, in big contrast to the morose gathering that took place in Canada, the declining G-7. Why don't you give us your thoughts on that, the difference between these two summits?

A New Spirit in the World, But in Europe?

Zepp-LaRouche: The SCO summit is the result of a conscious effort to create a more human world, and I really think that the fact that—as we discussed it already on this show—Modi and Xi Jinping have reset the policy between India and China; that Pakistan and India, under the umbrella of the SCO, can now talk about issues, is a wonderful development as well. The whole dynamic is one of cooperation, mutual trust, and how countries should relate to each other; that such relations are normal.

Thirty-four years ago, I created the Schiller Institute, with the idea that we need a new foreign policy; that nations should relate to the best traditions of each other, and not the worst. And that is what I see now. You have a deep discussion about the fundamental principles of each culture. In China, you have Confucius and Mencius, who were both mentioned by Xi Jinping; in India, you have the Vedic tradition, the Gupta period, you have the Indian Renaissance—much of this was referred to by Modi in his previous speech at the June 1-3 Shangri-La Dialogue in Singapore.

These leaders understand that you have to look for

the most profound image of man in their respective cultures, and politics follows out of that. Out of Confucius, the ideal of eternal learning, of life-long learning and character improvement comes the harmony in the family. And out of harmonious families comes harmony in the nation, and among nations as well. Similarly in the Indian philosophy, is the idea of a cosmic order, which should guide our behavior on the planet—the idea of *ahimsa*, that man has to educate himself up to the point that he is incapable of having any harmful thought.

G-7 Heads of State Summit.

Now, this happens to be the same idea you find in Nicholas of Cusa, or Leibniz or Schiller—Schiller's conception of the beautiful soul. That kind of thinking is almost completely absent in the Western world right now, certainly absent in the G-7, or Macron's G-6 against 1, or perhaps better said the G-4. There are only four countries left that are absolutely determined to keep the sanctions against Russia and similar things—Germany, France, Great Britain and Canada: It's not exactly a strong alliance.

The contrast between the SCO meeting and the really catastrophic failure of the G-7 summit could not be more obvious. The fact that the G-7 countries can only be negative, and are also having huge fights among themselves, is a reflection that this old order is collapsing, and it's collapsing very fast. One big area where you can see the collapse is the refugee crisis in Europe, which has come back in full force.

Schlanger: How significant is it that Trump brought up bringing Russia back into the G-7 to make it the G-8 again?

Zepp-LaRouche: Well, you know, Putin was very funny. He said he would invite the next G-7 to have their next meeting to Moscow. But I don't think Russia is putting a huge

Matteo Salvini, Italian Interior Minister.

priority on being part of something that is clearly not the most dynamic model in the world. Much more important for Russia at this point is the orientation towards Asia.

Foreign Minister Lavrov made an important point after the Singapore meeting, saying that to guarantee that this process succeeds, the six power talks have to be restarted. That would involve the two Koreas, Japan, China, the United States, and Russia. I think that that is absolutely to the point.

I think that the whole situation will change because you have now complete disunity in Europe. There are now two new governments that are absolutely in favor of restoring relations with Russia. One is Austria, which just hosted a very important summit for President Putin; and the other is the new Italian government, where Deputy Prime Minister Matteo Salvini just called for an alliance with Russia to fight terrorism, saying that you cannot deal with extremism in all its forms unless you cooperate with Russia.

This is all changing very rapidly, and I wouldn't be surprised if things get much more turbulent in Europe and more changes occur. One can only hope that they go in the direction of cooperating with the New Silk Road and not in the direction of chaos, which is also an imminent possibility.

Change the Policy Towards Africa

Schlanger: You mentioned the refugee crisis, which is back on the front burner, even though it's not at the same numbers as it was a couple of years ago. What's happening with this? How has this become an issue once again?

Zepp-LaRouche: First of all, there are many refugees now, because the weather had been bad for some time; now that it's better, a great number of refugees are lining up, waiting to be put in boats by human traffickers. One ship, the *Aquarius*, and its 600 passengers, was just refused entry at a port in Italy; then there was a huge brawl, because Macron attacked the Italian government because of it. And then the Italians referred to the high horse Macron was sitting on, given that they, the French, had had terrible treatment of tens of thousands of refugees over the years. Finally, Macron and Italian Prime Minister Conte talked on the telephone, and a state visit was scheduled for Friday, June 15. We'll have to see how that goes. The 600 refugees were finally accepted by the new Spanish government of Prime Minister Sánchez.

But, what happens when the next ship arrives? The refugee crisis has now led to a huge crisis in the coalition government in Germany. Horst Seehofer, Germany's Interior Minister, who had been the Bavarian Minister President, wanted to present his master plan. Merkel basically forbid him to, whereupon Seehofer and Chancellor Kurz from Austria, and Italian Deputy Prime Minister Salvini, all got on the telephone. Kurz talked about a "coalition of the willing" to agree to turn refugees back at the border if they're already registered in any one European country. German Chancellor Merkel, on the other hand, together with the Social Democratic Party (SPD), wants to find a Europe-wide solution.

This has created complete turmoil, because only three members of parliament of Merkel's own CDU party are backing her. The SPD, on the other hand, says, if Merkel capitulates to Seehofer, they may call for a vote of confidence and new elections. So this is highly unstable. I cannot see how either of these solutions could function. If you close the external EU borders—that's what they want, to make a "Fortress Europe," to increase the coast guard, to make sure that no refugees can come in, it can't function. And if you close the internal borders, there goes the Schengen Agreement, and that was the basis on which the euro

Professor Michele Geraci.

actually was possible, because if you don't have open borders within Europe, a common currency doesn't make sense.

So I think this thing could explode at any moment. All of these ideas are unworkable, and are a reflection of the fact that these establishments just don't understand that the only way to solve the refugee crisis in a human way, is via the large-scale infrastructure and industrial development of all of Africa. China has already begun doing that. So, were the European governments intelligent, they would just say: We'll accept China's offer to cooperate in large-scale infrastructure and other development plans for Africa—to create an incentive for all the young people in Africa, who will then decide to stay home and build their countries, rather than risk their lives crossing the Sahara and dying of thirst, or crossing the Mediterranean and drowning.

We have to change the policy towards Africa if we want to solve this problem.

They Must Humble Themselves and Reconsider

Schlanger: And Helga, on that note, it does appear there are people in the Italian government who are making that point. One of the new ministers, Prof. Michele Geraci has a document out in which he talks about this idea of Italy, and other European countries, working with China to provide the infrastructure and create the means by which people can stay in their homes and actually have a future.

What else do you see as far as a positive part of the transformation of Europe in the emergence of this new Italian government?

Zepp-LaRouche: There was first the appointment of ministers, several of whom have very decent positions on Glass-Steagall, on the creation of a national bank, on renegotiating the Maastricht Treaty conditions, rejecting austerity in favor of an investment program. So there are many interesting points. This new coalition government is not completely unproblematic, because there are also many greenie ideas in it.

The second round of people have now been appointed to the undersecretary minister positions, and there you have—I don't know the total number—but about 6 or 10 of them have signed an appeal by Movisol (our sister organization in Italy) to President Trump, asking him to implement Glass-Steagall.

I expect, given that the financial system is in a very precarious condition, once this new Italian government consolidates, which it is in the process of doing right now, that you will see a lot more motion towards Glass-Steagall.

Glass-Steagall and the laws of the European Union are, at this current moment, legally incompatible. But it's a very promising development. One reflection that good things are going on, is that the EU representative for the negotiation of the Brexit, former Belgian Prime Minister Guy Verhofstadt, just came out with a huge attack on several leading European political figures. He said that the following people are stooges of Russian President Putin: UK Independence Party leader Nigel Farage, Marine Le Pen in France, Salvini, and Hungarian Prime Minister Viktor Orban. He also launched vicious attacks against Trump. There are already some people now suing him, and you cannot just claim that somebody is a stooge and paid agent, when they are not.

You can see the freakout level is really quite big. I think the potential is also there, given the fact that there is now a motion towards cooperation with Russia coming from several places in Europe. There is also some softening. Some people are reviewing the situation and saying: Look, there is the biggest infrastructure development in history. The rules are already being rewritten. The new WTO will be written by the New Silk

Guy Verhofstadt, European Parliament's Brexit negotiator.

Road. Why not join it and profit from all of these developments? The hidden champions in the European *Mittelstand* and others, have so much to contribute to solve the problems of this world. Rather than retreating into a Fortress Europe and trying to keep every foreigner out, we should change the policy.

The time has come to realize that all the arrogant people, who claim to be the best and the brightest, really aren't not so smart at all. They don't want to acknowledge that their neo-liberal, neo-con, geopolitical system is going under. It's going under because it favors only the elite, a financial elite—an establishment. It is harmful to the majority of the people. The new models, the New Silk Road, the Shanghai Cooperation Organization model, and the BRICS model, all of these are more attractive, especially to the people of the developing countries. The West would do much better to say, "OK, we have to rethink what we are doing. Maybe we can reinvent ourselves if we cooperate with this new dynamic."

The breakthrough of Singapore has created an example that this can be done! You can change history if you want to, and if you have the will, and if you have good intentions. People should follow this example.

Grant Us Peace

Schlanger: There's one other place where change is needed, and that is the continuing war on the people of Yemen coming from the Saudi Arabian government and the United Arab Emirates—with some support from the United States and the United Kingdom. There's a battle underway right now for the port city of Hodeidah, where there was a bombing of a Doctors Without Borders hospital. This is the port where most of the food comes into the country, and it's already a country where 60% of the people are food insecure.

Helga, what can be done? Some Congressmen have signed a letter calling for an immediate move for an "Authorization for the Use of Military Force" (AUMF) with the idea being that the United States *would not* participate in this, but would move to stop it.

This is something that also needs to be brought

before the people of the world, isn't it?

Zepp-LaRouche: Yes. Before this bombing of Hodeidah started, Yemen was characterized by the United Nations as the worst humanitarian catastrophe on the planet. The Russian Foreign Ministry has just commented on the fact that the bombing of this port has started, saying that this will make a political solution that much harder.

There is one country right now which really could stop it: That is the United States. If the United States would just make sure Saudi Arabia does not have the means to continue this, it would stop. I find it promising that two members of the Knesset, the Israeli parliament, commented on the Singapore summit, saying that this could be a model to solve the Middle East crisis, including the conflict between Saudi Arabia and Iran.

That is the right way to go; military solutions just don't function. At the beginning of the year I said that geopolitics must be overcome, because geopolitics is the basis of war. In the last century, it was the basis of two world wars. I think we have to come to a situation in which—given that nuclear weapons exist, which could lead to the annihilation of civilization—we have to move to a world where war is absolutely outlawed as a means of conflict resolution.

This is why I think now, with this changed dynamic, a summit between President Trump and President Putin is of absolute urgency. I know that a spokesman for the State Department said that both sides are looking at it, and looking at preparations—but I think it's very urgent. I think this idea that the Middle East must find an approach similar to that used in the Korea situation, is absolutely to the point.

Schlanger: Well, on that point, I'd like to finish by asking you to say something about this wonderful conference this past weekend in New York City sponsored by the Schiller Institute, on the theme, "Dona Nobis Pacem." You participated in it. What are your thoughts about how this kind of event points the way to this change of the New Silk Road Spirit taking over?

Zepp-LaRouche: I think it was a quite successful conference. There was a student meeting on Friday, with U.S. students for the New Silk Road. On Saturday, we had a very important conference where we had the Deputy Permanent Representative of the Russian

Schiller Institute

Dmitry Polyanskiy, Russia's First Deputy Permanent Representative to the UN.

Federation to the United Nations as one of the speakers. I think it was very important for people to see and hear him—to see that Russians are not the creatures portrayed by the *New York Times*. They are human beings who have a good sense of humor and have a lot to give. We had a lot of strategic discussion over the day.

On Sunday, we were treated to a beautiful concert, with African-American Spirituals and Beethoven's *Mass in C Major*, performed by the Schiller Institute Chorus. The church in which the concert took place was completely full. Everyone was really inspired with the understanding that Classical culture is needed to elevate people to bring out the most noble aspects of humanity. In that spirit, you can solve any problem.

So I will ask you, once again: Join the Schiller Institute, become part of the Renaissance movement, and help us to bring forward the Silk Road Spirit; or as they said in the Shanghai Cooperation Organization meeting, the "Shanghai Spirit." This spirit is really the spirit of Confucius, and Mencius, and Schiller, and Leibniz. Help us bring forward this spirit in the Western world. We will all profit from it.

Schlanger: With that, I think we'll conclude. Thank you very much, Helga, and we'll see you next week.

Zepp-LaRouche: Yes, till next week.

SCHILLER INSTITUTE BEETHOVEN CONCERT

Classical Music Properly Understood Can Stop War

by Dennis Speed and Diane Sare

I do not like to talk about my mass, or, generally, about myself, but I believe that I have treated the text as it has seldom been treated before.
— *Ludwig van Beethoven*

June 18—Although the June 12 United States/North Korea Summit in Singapore was still two days away, the intention of the Schiller Institute's June 10 concert, entitled *Dona Nobis Pacem: 1968-2018*, prepared the 450 persons in attendance, and the 150 choral and orchestral members performing, not only for that impending, successful shift of history, but for the possibility of similar changes in the immediate future. The revolutionary thinking required to make such breakthroughs is the subject of Beethoven's *Mass in C Major.* The Schiller Institute NYC Chorus and Orchestra has begun a study of this work, and presented its preliminary findings on it in performance.

As Music Director John Sigerson pointed out in the program essay he provided for the occasion, "A Concert Dedicated to the Spirit of RFK, Beethoven, and the New Paradigm":

Indeed, Beethoven once commented to a friend that if people took seriously the discovered principles embedded in his compositions, warfare within and among nations would become an impossibility.

Eleanor Eng

Schiller Institute NYC Chorus performing at the Dona Nobis Pacem concert in New York City, June 10, 2018.

The Schiller Institute has embarked upon a mission to present little-performed, but important, Classical compositions that are generally considered outside the competence of amateur choruses. They are, nonetheless, essential to the cultural literacy of all thinking American citizens. The Institute also seeks to perform such works, whenever possible complete with orchestra, at the scientific tuning of C = 256 cycles per second. No one else in America is presently doing this.

It had been proposed three years ago by Institute co-founder Lyndon LaRouche to recruit, in New York City, a 1500-person chorus which studies the Italian *bel canto* voice-placement principles and, based on the insights thus gained, begins to "think like Beethoven." Beethoven's hypothesis, that his music, properly understood, can stop war, should be rigorously tested "in the street" through the social practice of choral presentation. This is particularly necessary at this time, when the United States so desperately needs to instantaneously change course and abandon the culture of death that has temporarily gripped the nation, but which runs counter to its original national purpose and mission.

The Concert

Schiller Institute representative Dennis Speed welcomed the audience with this message:

This concert is the conclusion of a conference that began yesterday, held in the context of a national state of reflection upon the 50th anniversary of the double assassinations of Martin Luther King and Robert F. Kennedy. Ludwig van Beethoven's *Mass in C Major* is the featured musical commentary we offer upon this occasion. As pointed out by conductor John Sigerson in the program, Beethoven, while composing the "Dona Nobis Pacem" section of the *Missa Solemnis,* the Solemn High Mass, wrote in his sketch-book: "Strength of sentiments of inner peace above all else ... Victory!"

"Death is swallowed up in victory! O grave, where is thy victory? O Death, where is thy sting?" says Saint Paul. So says Beethoven also, and so say we today, reflecting upon Martin Luther King, Robert Kennedy and many others. Paul also, however, adds, in a passage that some find mysterious, "For the sting of death is sin; and the strength of sin is the Law." Is it not a law, that all of us must die? How can we then be truly free? Friedrich Schiller, in his various discussions of the Sublime, points out that "even the beautiful must die" and that if man is not fully free from the tyranny of death, then he is truly not free at all. Life itself would then be a tragedy.

But it is not. Our lives are not contained within our skins, our exteriors. Through creativity, our lives are contained not only in some other human beings, but in all of humanity, all of creation itself. We represent not only a physical presence in the world, but a principle of creation simultaneously contained within but also beyond the physical world as such. That universal principle is growth, and it is manifested in all things as progress. Its human manifestation is called wealth. It is from the ennoblement of the mind and character of mankind, that all other permanent forms of wealth, including the physical well-being of the whole human race, will flow. The real poverty of our time begins with a poverty of the soul. That poverty of soul, and its accompanying physical poverty, is not an inevitable objective condition, but a thoroughly unnecessary subjective choice.

After the invocation, delivered by St. Anthony of Padua's Father Mario F. Julian, the concert was begun by violinist Brenden Zak, 19 years of age, who played the "Andante" section of Bach's Violin Sonata No. 2 in A Minor.

Speed then introduced two speeches, given within 24 hours of each other, by Martin Luther King and Robert Kennedy, on April 3 and April 4, 1968. Both speeches were prophetic. King's "I've Been to the Mountaintop" is one of the most quoted and best known in American history. Kennedy's extemporaneous speech the evening following King's assassination, is one of the least. Kennedy's two references to Aeschylus, the Greek tragedian of 2,500 years earlier, were essential to his changing the despairing direction of thought of the African-American audience to whom he spoke that night in Indianapolis, showing, as did King's "Gethsemane" speech of the night before, the power of immortality over death.

The African-American Spirituals, *Ain'a That Good News*, arranged by William Dawson, and *Honor! Honor!* arranged by Hall Johnson, followed, conducted

Schiller Institute NYC Chorus and Orchestra performing at the Dona Nobis Pacem Concert in New York City, June 10, 2018.

by Diane Sare. Sare has worked over the years with Johnson's close associate Eugene Simpson, who provided crucial commentary and biographical material on Johnson for the Program, and is the author of *Hall Johnson: His Life, His Spirit, and His Music* (Scarecrow Press, 2008).

"Poverty is a form of violence" was the title of the next section's Kennedy/King remarks, read by Speed. The excerpt, taken from Kennedy's April 5, 1968 Cleveland address, "The Mindless Menace of Violence," unaltered, could have been as productively stated today:

> Some Americans who preach nonviolence abroad, fail to practice it here at home. Some who accuse others of inciting riots, have by their own conduct, invited them.
>
> Some look for scapegoats, others look for conspiracies, but this much is clear: violence breeds violence, repression brings retaliation, and only a cleaning of our whole society can remove this sickness from our soul.
>
> For there is another kind of violence, slower but just as deadly, destructive as the shot or the bomb in the night. This is the violence of institutions; indifference, and inaction, and slow decay. This is the violence that afflicts the poor, that poisons relations between men because their skin has different colors. This is a slow destruction of a child by hunger, and schools without books and homes without heat in the winter.
>
> This is the breaking of a man's spirit by denying him the chance to stand as a father and as a man among other men. And this too afflicts us all.

The chorus brought this section of the program to its conclusion with three Spirituals: *Lord, I Don't Feel No-Ways Tired* and *I'll Never Turn Back No Mo*, arranged by Johnson; and *Daniel, Daniel, Servant of the Lord*, arranged by Undine S. Moore.

How Is It Possible?

In addition to the excited responses she received to the choral performances overall, conductor Diane Sare reported:

The church was filled with people who had heard about the concert in many different ways. Many members of the audience had been members of the chorus in past performances and therefore follow the chorus closely. About two thirds of the audience had attended previous events sponsored by the Foundation for the Revival of Classical Culture, featuring the Schiller Institute NYC Chorus. Many people came from the powerful images on the poster, which they had seen somewhere. The Harlem Opera Theater, directed by Gregory Hopkins, got the word out to its audience, many of whom attended. The audience very much reflected the diversity of the chorus.

Sare pointed out that while soloists Sarah Abigail Griffths (soprano), Linda Childs (alto), Gregory Hopkins (tenor) and Paul An (bass) stood out in this day's performance, it was the development of the "richness of sound" of the chorus—what some musicians have referred to as the "warmth" of the voices—that was most distinct. When tenor Reginald Bouknight sang his solo parts for three of the five African-American Spirituals presented by the chorus, the unity of effect achieved by the contrast between his "call," and the chorus's "response," was greatly assisted by the proper tuning of the voices.

The answer to the often asked question, "How is it possible for the Schiller Institute's musical efforts and performances to be distinctly superior to many professional and nearly all other non-professional choruses in the United States?" does not lie in the musical training, practice, choral personnel selection, or the music itself. It lies behind, underneath, and above the music. A 45-year emphasis by Lyndon LaRouche on the role of Classical composition, particularly Beethoven's compositional method, in clearing the mind to establish necessary mental conditions for true original creative work, has informed the work of director John Sigerson.

Sigerson, as a vocalist, instrumentalist, and a member of the team that worked with LaRouche in the 1980s to produce the book, *A Manual on the Rudiments of Tuning and Registration: Introduction and Human Singing Voice,* helped to rediscover the scientific basis for the tuning of all musical instruments in congruence with the human voice, and the entire "vocal registral palette" ranging from soprano to bass. This application of and experimentation with the *bel canto* methods well known during the time of the Italian Renaissance, is informed by the far more advanced compositional principles of Beethoven; this provides an intention, a "reason for being" for these particular performances, which are done as proofs of principle, not as "highbrow entertainments," or as "cultural wallpaper," mere background for purposes completely unrelated to music.

Classical Composition Is a Way of Life

The method of Classical composition is not a technique, but a way of life. It is the essential tool by means of which human immortality may be deployed as an efficient ordering principle, properly evaluating the importance and the role of truth in the day–to-day affairs of life. The matters of our lives, and our decisions, are thus raised to the level of current history, as opposed to being relegated to the non-existent, wholly illusory realm of "current events," forgotten almost before they occur.

For citizens who would save their nation and civilization, by building something new and unprecedented with the people of Asia and the world, these concert studies and performances are "experiments in truth," much like those carried out by Mahatma Gandhi and Martin Luther King: They are the highest expression of "creative non-violent direct action"—but action on the minds of the participants. This supplies an urgent, sometimes even unconscious, sense of mission for the participating vocalists and instrumentalists—all transformed into musicians—that is unavailable to nearly all conventional ensembles. This precedes each performance, and determines each performance's success.

We now stand poised upon the threshold of a new cultural paradigm, expressed in the worldwide economic revolution called the New Silk Road. It is in fact a victory secured through the decades of the relentless composing, and work of Schiller Institute Founder Helga Zepp-LaRouche, and her husband, economist Lyndon LaRouche. And the living musical metaphor of that new cultural paradigm is the struggle and triumph of the deaf Beethoven, the deaf composer who knew and proved that music fundamentally exists in an unheard realm, behind, beneath and above the notes.

The Case of Sir Isaac Newton—or, What Was God Thinking?

by David Shavin

Editor's Foreword

In order to understand David Shavin's article below, the reader must become aware that he or she has (in almost all cases) been hoodwinked by widespread and nasty propaganda for a radically false view of what science is. If science were really the impossible chimera which it is claimed to be by the generality of our prestigious and non-so-prestigious media and academic institutions, then we would never have advanced to more truthful understandings of "man and nature," nor advanced our cultural and material civilization as we have done, as mankind, ever since our first entrance onto the stage of the universe millions of years ago.

To jump ahead here: to those who claim that it is "Newton" who was responsible for our ability to launch earth satellites and moon-landings, we will show that these achievements owe precisely nothing whatever to Newton.

Resuming the thread of our discussion: What exactly is this false view of "science" which must be exploded? One of the difficulties of defining it, is that it so saturates all our discourse to the exclusion of any possible alternative, that it seems at first that there is really nothing there to be defined. It seems at first that this false view of science is self-evident. Think here of the difficulties Eighteenth-century chemists had in reasoning through the properties of gases (mass, for instance), when they were only just beginning to work out the implications of the fact that each of them had actually spent his entire lifetime at the bottom of a vast sea of gas.

For initial, working definitions of the pseudo-science which everywhere surrounds us in the abused name of science, let us give two. One was actually proposed as a definition of "science" by some benighted person (I forget who), who wrote that "science is the mathematical description of natural phenomena." This was the bastard creed of that British author who prefaced a London edition of Benjamin Franklin's path-breaking work on electricity, with the statement that it was not science because it contained no equations.

A kindred, false, definition of "science" is the lowly one of "curve-fitting." I must admit that "curve-fitting" doesn't sound quite so prestigious as a job-description—but isn't it really the same thing as that first definition in the last analysis?

But before we can make any more headway here, we first have to go back to deal with the nitty-gritty of the reader's (most readers') actual life-experience of the distinctions we are trying to make here. The reason they feel impelled to defend the fraud, e.g., of Newtonian physics, is not because they have mastered it for themselves. It is because they fail to master it. Or better, they believe they "have failed"—as in "you flunk this course." They defend a caste-distinction all the more strongly, as one that they have tried, but failed to achieve for themselves. Even if they got good grades, they still know inwardly that they lack real knowledge. But all the more do they believe that this sort of knowledge must be out there somewhere—if not in their teacher, then in his teacher's teacher. It's all known, all of it—I'm certain of it! There are those who know it. Let's call them "the Cathar elect."

A corollary is that current scientific (mis-)education teaches that everything is known (at least in principle). This is reinforced by only giving students problems which were already solved long ago, perhaps by using the same simple-minded methods they have just been taught. Descartes even tried to limit the very definition of "problem" to only *those* problems! But the truth is that very little is yet known—as Dmitry Mendeleyev was at pains to point out in the preface to his great elementary chemistry textbook. The farce of so-called "dark matter" provides a ludicrous example. Many galaxies do not behave as they should according to Newtonian (ahem!) principles. Does this anomaly mean there is something "out there" that we do not yet understand? Not at all! It can only be more *matter* that we have been unable to detect—the Newtonian principles must stand! But this so-called "matter" cannot be seen, felt, touched, tasted…? Certainly the real, historical Isaac Newton, Newton the black magician, would be happy with this so-called "matter."

But now we must ask what is science actually—real, true science? It exists, and it is provably effective, but I cannot even begin to give anything like an adequate answer to that question—at least within the limits of this preface. David Shavin truly indicates how the bare-bones algebraic formulas which were falsely claimed as Newton's discoveries, were only dumbed-down, impoverished hacks of results which had been achieved earlier, and much more fully and usefully, by Kepler and Leibniz respectively—using methods which the Newtonians openly reviled. David

also rightly asks whether light is alive, and whether matter is alive. In truth, there is no abiotic universe of physics—there is only the one existing universe. In it, the principle of life and the principle of creative mentation are everywhere active, and Max Planck truly said that you cannot get behind or beyond consciousness, even in the smallest particle—if such particle were possible. This is the hylozoic monism of Plato and his successors.

Plato's greatest living successor is now, and has long been Lyndon H. LaRouche, Jr., who wrote in an article that we have recently reprinted here, that the most fundamental principle of science is the absolute distinction of the human species from all animals. To go further in the study of what real science is, you could do much worse than to begin reading his historic writings which are being republished here weekly.

In conclusion, let me say here that if there is any truth in these paragraphs above, the reader owes it all to that same Lyndon H. LaRouche, Jr.

—Tony Papert

How can one tell if a British imperialist is lying?
His mouth is open.

How can one tell if British imperialism is dying?
The stiff upper lip drops and the lying spews out of control.

Introduction

June 13—There are some individuals one meets in life, where lying is not the exception to the rule, but is the rule; and the chief fear that one has in confronting such a person on a given lie, is that, inevitably, the next day an even bigger whopper will be the result.

The recent period has witnessed the one boldly ridiculous lie after another, coming out of those formerly "stiff upper-lip" fellows associated with the British Empire. The cases that jump to mind go by the name of the "Steele Dossier," the "Skripal Affair," and the "Syrian White Helmet video series." As the lock-step control over their "dump American giant" has come un-

Isaac Newton

glued, the feebleness of their vaunted methods is exposed. The appropriate image is the scene at the end of "The Wizard of Oz," where the all-powerful wizard is unmasked. Behind the screen, and the smoke and mirrors, is a rather pathetic individual.

Enter Isaac Newton—perhaps the epitome, and the central image, of British imperial lying from the beginning. Here we present the completely overlooked story of Newton's so-called "solution" of the Brachistochrone Contest, where the Newton lie was most completely exposed. In reading this story, the reader would best be advised to forget any impressions he or she might have picked up along the way regarding a so-called Newton-Leibniz controversy as to who first developed the calculus.[1] That whole controversy was manufactured as a reaction to Newton's embarrassing failure in the 1697 Brachistochrone Contest. It became the central cause of the wild flight-forward assault against Gottfried Leibniz, the strategic development that doomed the Empire and made the American Revolution necessary.[2]

I. Newton's Bluff

In May and June of 1696, Gottfried Leibniz and Jean Bernoulli initiated a public scientific contest around the unpacking of the workings of gravity. The question was quite general: What path would a particle trace out if it were to fall under its own weight, taking the least time (that is, brachisto-chronos, or shortest-time) to go from a higher point to any given lower point?[3] However, the solution was quite particular. Even more important than a correct solution was the method behind the solution, and Bernoulli promised that the working out of the solution involved a wealth of riches for the developments at the core of the calculus.

However, Isaac Newton, the supposed master of gravity and inventor of the calculus, not only did not have a clue, but in fact emitted a response that deserves to be on the all-time list of bloopers and buffoonery. Even worse, for the last three centuries, no one is supposed to point out that the emperor is not wearing any clothes. However, given the behavior of recent emissions from the British establishment, perhaps an unblinking look is long overdue.

Early in 1697, Newton sent his supposed solution to his sponsor, Sir Charles Montague, the head of the Royal Society and the founder of the Bank of England. Newton drew a cycloid, and then he showed that it can be enlarged to pass through the designated point. That is it. No explanation as to why or whether the cycloid solves the problem, no new methods developed, no joyful wealth of developments.

It is difficult to convey how ridiculous Newton's

submission is, but there is a joke passed around by math teachers of note. A right triangle is drawn with the two smaller sides labeled with lengths 3 cm and 4 cm, while the unknown side—longest side, the hypotenuse—is labeled "x".

The instruction for the student is, "Find x." (Students who learned their Pythagorean Theorem know how to add the square of 3, which is 9, to the square of 4, which is 16, and get the sum of 25. They then take the square root of 25 to get the value of x as 5.) However, this clueless—though bold—student tries to bluff his

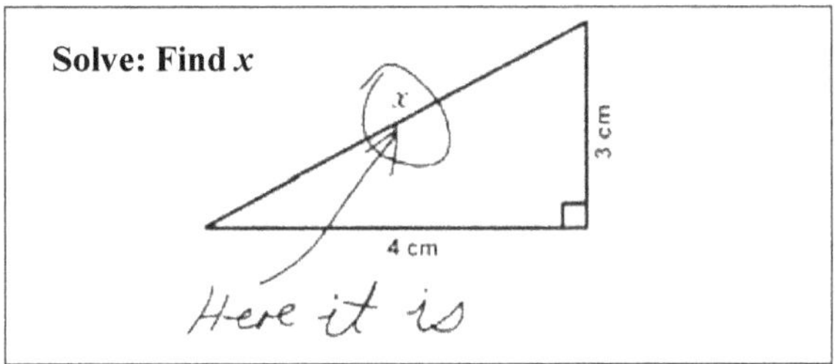

way through, simply circling the "x" and answering the teacher, "Here it is!"

Surely, Isaac Newton deserves better than this, wouldn't you think? Let's examine his actual complete submission, the one that Montague had published anonymously in the 1697 *Philosophical Transactions*, the

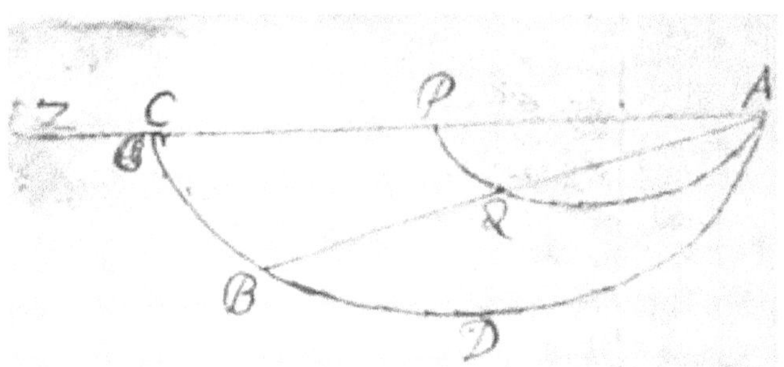

Newton's diagram from his letter to Lord Montague.

periodical of the British Royal Society. Hint: it looks a lot more imposing than it is!

"**Problem.** *It is required to find the curve ADB in which a weight, by the force of its gravity, shall descend most swiftly from any given point A to any given point B.*

"**Solution.** *From the given point A let there be drawn an unlimited straight line APCZ parallel to the horizontal, and on it let there be described an arbitrary cycloid AQP meeting the straight line AB (assumed drawn and produced if necessary) in the point Q, and further a second cycloid ADC whose base and height are to the base and height of the former as AB is to AQ respec-*

---

1. First, Newton never understood the full-blown power of Leibniz' "analysis situs" method, which developed the powerful inverse relationship of differentiation and integration. Second, Leibniz, and many others, had no trouble understanding Newton's limited calculation tricks. Newton was certainly not alone in developing and extending such techniques.

2. H. Graham Lowry, *How the Nation Was Won—America's Untold Story 1630-1754.* Available as epub, Kindle, or PDF.

3. In the reduced case of the lower point lying directly underneath the upper point, the workings of gravity are not made explicit.

tively. This last cycloid will pass through the point B, and it will be that curve along which a weight, by the force of its gravity, shall descend most swiftly from the point A to the point B. QEI (what was to be found) "[4]

That really is it. Don't be fooled by the hand-waving. Newton drew a horizontal line, hung a small cycloid from it, and then demonstrated he could enlarge that cycloid to a larger cycloid, one that could include both the starting point A and the end point B. He could just as well have drawn a squiggly line from A to B. There is no clue as to why he is drawing a cycloid, nor is any method demonstrated.

What Newton has effectively said here is: "My solution? Draw a cycloid curve from A to B. Oh, that's too obvious? I'll generalize that for you. Draw a cycloid anywhere and I can move it so that it connects A and B." It is even sillier, when one considers that the problem as posed never required B to be any special distance from A, simply at a lower level. The only "method" Newton displayed was in answer to a trivial matter that had nothing to do with the problem.

Perhaps the kid who circled the "x" should have demonstrated that his method was quite powerful, because it could be generalized so as to be made capable of circling not just "x," but any letter of the alphabet desired!

For over three centuries, Newton's promoters have lauded this solution as proof of the superior power of his mind, and as the perfect reproach to Leibniz and Bernoulli for ever daring to challenge Newton. Let's put this buffoonery in context. Don't worry about the mathematical formulas; an accounting of the core of the brachistochrone puzzle will be provided in Section V.

II. How Did Poor Newton Find Himself in this Awkward Situation?

Isaac Newton was a talented youth who, early on in his career, took a dark path. Today, as a first approximation, one might think of victims of video-games, who deem themselves all-powerful in their fantasy world. "A mind is," indeed, "a terrible thing to waste." In this case, it led Newton into some uncomfortable career choices.

In 1684, Newton was chosen, by those who would turn England into an Empire, to craft a counter to the developments in science on the continent of Europe by Johannes Kepler and Gottfried Leibniz. At that point in life, the forty-one-year-old Newton had been for all his life a loner, whose primary work had been an obsessive and isolated search for the alchemical mysteries (whereby, e.g., one could manufacture gold from cheaper constituents). He had also mastered many computational and approximation techniques.

Edmund Halley[5] visited Newton, proposing that he reduce to a mathematical system Kepler's beautiful and harmonic physical-science development of the solar system—where the sun's role, involving nothing less than light, heat, radiation, rotation, magnetism and the pull of gravity, was all one dynamic whole.[6] Could Newton reduce the sun's activity to an inverse square law, an equation where the pull of the sun on a planet diminished by a constant number times the inverse of the square of the distance? For example, the pull at a million miles away would calculate as four times as much pull, two million miles away.

The Euclid Method—Hide the Cow But Get the Milk

This was a time-honored project to market the results of a scientific breakthrough while simultaneously obscuring and covering up the very real creative mentation that created the breakthrough. The classic case was Euclid's reduction of the achievements of two centuries of Pythagoreans and Platonists, notably including Theaetetus' development of the mutual harmonies of 'objective' space and 'subjective' hearing.[7] Sounds complicated, but anyone who has ever had to blindly follow step-by-step instructions with no overview, but where the lawyers had more to do with the wording than the engineers, might approximate the issue involved here. In Newton's case, the regularities of the solar system, including the workings of gravitational pull, would be simplified to the interplay of two objects at a certain distance—and the poor student is left with some magical force acting over some distance through some evac-

---

4. Letter of Newton to Montague.

5. The story of the breaking and recruitment of Halley to anti-science activities is one that involved the mysterious 1679 fire where all of Johannes Kepler's manuscripts were stored. See: http://por-la-glass-steagall.blogspot.com/2014/ 02/the-transit-of-venus-or-cranes-of.html

6. Johannes Kepler, *The Harmony of the World*, 1619.

7. An over-simplification, but Kepler developed how the known bodies of the solar system were arranged in harmonic coherence with the musical scale, a project set out in Plato's *Timaeus* dialogue.

uated space. Newton took the assignment, and in 1687 delivered his *The Mathematical Principles of Natural Philosophy*—for short, the *Principia*.

Leibniz responded to this mathematizing operation by developing Kepler's solar dynamics further in his 1688/9 "Essay on the Cause of the Celestial Motions." In short, this led directly into the consolidation of his alliance with the Bernoulli brothers, and to intensive work on the physical, transcendental curves—particularly the cycloid, the catenary, and the brachistochrone. In the case of the cycloid, Newton's public posture had usefully provoked scientific developments that threatened his role, and were a boon for the world!

'Would Someone Close the Window?'

The reclusive Newton did not take easily to his new public role. The *Principia* project put him forward as the leading scholar of England's 1688/9 "Glorious Revolution," and Newton's rabid anti-Catholicism put him into the new Parliament. There Newton suffered in silence, evidently too terrified to speak. The only speech recorded of Newton during his tenure in Parliament was a one-liner, to the effect: "Would someone close the window?" He left Parliament in 1689, plunged into his alchemical musings, suffered apparent rejection by his dear Fatio de Duillier, and spent most of 1693 in mental disarray.

It wasn't until Lord Charles Montague, the founder of the Bank of England in 1694, appointed him to the Royal Mint in 1696 that Newton found solid footing again. He particularly relished tracking down counterfeiters and executing them. As of the June 1696 Brachistochrone Contest, Newton's passion was not related to the contest's goal of the betterment of mankind through the pushing forward of scientific boundaries— but he had allowed himself to be put forward as the great thinker of England. Hence, he found himself in a rather awkward situation.

III. Why Didn't Newton Simply Ignore the Contest?

God knows, he certainly tried to.

In brief, Leibniz and Bernoulli forced the issue, as follows. In June 1696, Johann Bernoulli published in the well-known *Acta Eruditorum*, the scientific journal founded by Leibniz, an article on how Leibniz's calculus was the appropriate new invention to tackle and solve the gaps in classical geometry. At the conclusion of that article, Bernoulli offered the example of the brachistochrone problem: What pathway would a particle trace out, in the shortest time, when falling only under its own weight from a higher position to any lower position? That is, how does gravity work? Newton had provided, in 1687, an equation to model the effects of the otherwise unknown gravity; Leibniz and Bernoulli had developed more powerful analytic techniques to begin unpacking how fundamental, though otherwise invisible, actions in nature work.

Bernoulli stressed that the solution was highly valuable, both for the richness of the result and even more for the powerful development of analytic methods involved in drawing out the solution. Further, in telling mathematicians that the solution was one of a small grouping of very well-known curves, Bernoulli made clear that the answer was neither tricky nor obscure— and that guessing from a small group of curves really wasn't the point of the contest.

The deadline for the solution of the puzzle was given as the end of the year. Mathematicians at Oxford, long-time colleagues of Newton with a history of numerous communications, began working on the puzzle no later than September 1696. It is not likely that Newton was unaware of the contest for over half a year (from June 1696 until late January 1697), but that is his story.

The Puzzle Circulates Prior to First Deadline

Prior to the June 1696 publication, Bernoulli had more than a few communications with Leibniz on the development of the transcendental curves and of the accompanying calculus. It was no surprise to Bernoulli that Leibniz, in June, immediately upon reception of Bernoulli's letter, could provide a solution (developing the correct differential equation from the conditions of the puzzle). Leibniz commented that the problem was most beautiful, and that despite his schedule and obligations, it attracted him against his will. Of note, the first person that Leibniz made sure to send the problem to was his friend in Florence, Italy, Rudolf Christian von Bodenhausen. Leibniz encouraged him to work on it, as it was a matter of extraordinary beauty.[8]

---

8. Leibniz had visited Bodenhausen in Florence, Italy, in 1689, where he was the tutor of the sons of the Grand Duke, Cosimo III. Leibniz had just finished his work on Kepler's dynamics. The visit was also a likely occasion impelling Leibniz's work on the catenary, as he could not have missed the dome of the Florentine Cathedral, Il Duomo. (Bruce Director

Bernoulli had also sent the puzzle, in May, 1696, to Pierre Varignon in Paris for circulation to the mathematicians of France. Varignon reported that he was "immediately rebuffed by its difficulty" and that he was not aware of "anyone, of all those to whom I announced your problem who has resolved it." In July, Bernoulli writes to Leibniz that neither the French nor the British have been able to solve the puzzle.[9] As the December 31st deadline approached, it is known, from correspondence between two of the Newton's colleagues, John Wallis and David Gregory, that their efforts to provide a demonstration have failed. At this point, December 1696, Newton was content to choose silence as the best course of action.

Bernoulli Takes Aim at Newton

At this point, Bernoulli had received only two correct solutions—one from Leibniz and one from his older brother, Jacob. Leibniz requested Bernoulli to extend the deadline, and in the December, 1696 *Acta Eruditorum*, Bernoulli announced that the new deadline was going to be Easter, 1697. Furthermore, on January 1, 1697, he composed a leaflet on the contest, one that put Newton in the cross-hairs. He sent the leaflet, amongst other places, to the French *Journal des scavans* and the British *Philosophical Transactions*. But he also made a point to have one delivered directly to Newton, taking away any possible "hidey-hole." The leaflet, called the "Programma," began:

> To the sharpest mathematicians now flourishing throughout the world.... We are well assured that there is scarcely anything more calculated to rouse noble minds to attempt work conductive to the increase of knowledge than the setting of problems at once difficult and useful, by the solving of which they may attain to personal fame as it were by a specially unique way, and raise for themselves enduring monuments with

posterity. For this reason, I ... propose to the most eminent analysts of this age, some problem, by means of which, as though by a touchstone, they might test their own methods, apply their powers, and share with me anything they discovered, in order that each might thereupon receive his due meed of credit when I publically announce the fact.

The fact is that half a year ago in the June number of the Leipzig *Acta*, I proposed such a problem whose usefulness linked with beauty will be seen by all who successfully apply themselves to it.... Only the celebrated Leibniz, who is so justly famed in the higher geometry has written me that he has by good fortune solved this, as he himself expresses it, very beautiful and hitherto unheard of problem....

Base and Venal Soul?

There was no way that Newton, or any other reader, could miss Bernoulli's explicit targeting of Newton in his "Programma": "Since nothing obscure remains, we earnestly request [mathematicians....] to bring to bear everything which they hold concealed in the final hiding places of their methods." Further, the prize is virtue, "not gold or silver, for these appeal only to base and venal souls from which we may hope for nothing laudable, nothing useful for science." (In 1696, Newton had finally attained his lucrative post as Warden of the Royal Mint.)[10] Rather the problem requires "solutions which are drawn from deep lying sources." Finally, in an unmistakable allusion to Newton's treatment of Kepler, the leaflet adds that "so few have appeared to solve our extraordinary problem even among those who boast that through special methods, which they commend so highly, they have not only penetrated the deepest secrets but also extended its boundaries in marvelous fashion; although their golden theorems... have been published by others long before."

Newton would recall this moment, bitterly, for years

---

develops LaRouche's discovery of the catenary-basis for the cupola: https://www.schillerinstitute.org/fid_02-06/031_long_life_catenary.html.) Regardless, it is known that Leibniz presented his new work on dynamics, work that, via Bodenhausen, might have influenced Stradivari's revolutionary "bel canto" violins (called the "Long Strads") presented to Cosimo III the following year.

9. "... nor the British." It is not known if any English mathematician communicated to Bernoulli directly. However, Bernoulli's younger brother, Hieronymus, was studying at Oxford and communicated with Johann. Hieronymus is thought to have been in touch with Wallis on the contest and would have known about the lack of progress.

10. Charles Montague, Chancellor of the Exchequer, set up the Bank of England in 1694 with the aid of John Locke. Over 1695/6, they established their team at the Royal Mint: Isaac Newton, Edmund Halley and Thomas Molyneaux. Were Locke's team Plato's philosopher-kings, organizing a republic? Unfortunately, they rather resembled hired sophists for an empire—more concerned about money manipulation than about production. Locke and Newton wrote dissertations on how to speculate on the relative valuations of gold and silver in various countries.

to come. In particular, in 1699, Newton interrupted his letter to Flamsteed to announce, seemingly out of the blue: "I do not love to be printed upon every occasion much less to be dunned and teased by foreigners about Mathematical things...."[11]

IV. Smoke and Mirrors

We are at one of those too rare moments when the imperial bullies get caught, having to fight on a battlefield which wasn't designed ahead of time in their favor. In other words, they have to fight out in the open—where they don't appear so unbeatable. An inspection of their shenanigans, under such circumstances, says a lot about what their methods were all along, when they had been hidden. In January, 1697, there is, indeed, a lot of pressure on Newton and Montague to respond. Here is where "Mr. Smoke and Mirrors" makes his appearance

The Surviving Cover Story

But first, one bit of housekeeping. Let us briefly, in two paragraphs, dispense with the more familiar cover story still used to this day: So the story goes, Newton came home from his important post at the Royal Mint one afternoon at 4 p.m., saw the challenge, and worked continuously until 4 a.m. the next morning to come up with his so-called "solution." That story—as with the other famous myth of the apple falling from a tree—was the product of public relations efforts some thirty years later.

The anecdote is alleged to be from the testimony of Newton's half-niece and housekeeper, Catherine Barton. However, since she was, at the time in question, neither in London nor his housekeeper, she did not, in fact, witness anything. At best, she was repeating what Newton himself had told her later on.[12] After Newton's demise in 1727, Catherine's husband, John Conduitt, in his role as a promoter of Newton's image, recorded the anecdote and cited his wife as the witness. (Conduitt was also Voltaire's source for the Newton "apple" story.) Further, that story is itself wholly dependent upon never actually looking at Newton's submission. Certainly, it would not have taken even twelve minutes, much less twelve hours, to come up with what Newton submitted.[13] Still, this story is the first thing brought up should anyone inquire about Newton and the Brachistochrone Contest. With that dispensed with, we turn to the shenanigans of 1697.

The Timing

There was a major effort to play with the timing of Newton's involvement with Bernoulli's challenge. Newton wrote on his copy of Bernoulli's leaflet, at some point, that he had received it on January 29, 1697, more than five weeks after it had been sent.[14]

Next, Newton's solution gives the appearance of being sent to his sponsor, Montague, the next day, on January 30th. However, the date on it was not in Newton's handwriting, and it was apparently added later. It is thought to be in the known script of Hans Sloane. Since Sloane was President of the Royal Society from 1727 to 1740, the period of time when Conduitt's "Newton-solved-it-overnight" story was born, it makes sense that the date was added to buttress the story.

Regardless, if the January 30th date is correct for the submission Newton sent to Montague, then there seems to be a delay of a couple of weeks in the normal procedure before the perfunctory reading to the Royal Society. Regardless, mid-February seems to be the first public event associated with Newton's non-solution. The minimal inference one can draw from all this is that it was at least an eight-week period from the sending of the "Programma" challenge to Newton's response. Hence, whatever time was eaten up by the delivery process, one can only guess that the rest of the time involved unsuccessful attempts to come up with a solution. It is most reasonable to assume that there were

---

11. Newton's clinical outburst on this matter was provoked by Flamsteed's mere reference to Jeremiah Horrocks. Newton knew that this young Keplerian genius of 1630's England had taken a serious and honest approach to Kepler. Mysteriously, in 1641 he dropped dead at age 22, and most of his papers were burned or lost. There was an attempt in England to revive Horrocks' work in the 1660's (Newton's student years). Newton joined up with those who would bury Horrocks for a second time. Hence, "Horrocks" was a trigger word for Newton. See: http://por-la-glass-steagall.blogspot.com/2014/02/the-transit-of-venus-or-cranes-of.html

12. Newton's care for his half-niece involved loaning her to his sponsor, Lord Montague, as his mistress. After Montague's death and his generous endowment left to Catherine, Newton married her to John Conduitt, whose own wealth had derived from his activities as Deputy Paymaster General for the British forces in Gibraltar. Otherwise, Conduitt inherited Newton's Master of the Mint position; and his noteworthy accomplishment in Parliament was to revoke the laws against witchcraft.

13. Perhaps the story had its roots in Newton's sensitivity to Bernoulli's published description that Leibniz had solved the puzzle immediately.

14. England's calendar was ten days behind Bernoulli's; so, Newton's January 29 was Bernoulli's February 8.

three to six weeks of deep anxiety. Yet, it gets "curiouser and curiouser."

The States of Mind of Newton and Montague

While Newton kept just about every worksheet and scrap paper throughout his life, it seems that no worksheet relating to his work on Bernoulli's challenge exists.[15] However, at least some of Newton's worksheets from this period do exist, and they reveal more than a little of the actual situation. There one finds Newton working on his alchemical transmutation of metals, where he explains that sulphur is "the most digested metal next to Gold, for tis Philaletha's King whose Brethren in their passage to him were taken prisoners r & are kept in bondage s by impure t & must be redeemed by his flesh & blood… For our crude sperm flows from a trinity of r immature s substances in one essence of which two (u & v) are extracted r out of ye earth of their nativity s by ye third ((u) & then become a pure milky virgin-like Nature drawn from ye menstruum of our sordid whore."[16]

It would be hard to make this stuff up … or even to want to do so. With such noise in his head, perhaps Newton was doing well merely to draw the picture of the cycloid.

Meanwhile, Montague publishes Newton's solution in the *Philosophical Transactions* for January, 1697 (though their monthly journal was, as a matter of course, published at least one or two months after the date). On the surface, the actions of Newton and Montague would seem to be a violation of the terms and spirit of the contest, as the actual solutions were awaiting an Easter deadline. However, since Newton's solution didn't actually give anybody a clue as to anything, it in fact made no difference to the actual contest; but it does speak to the state of mind of Montague and his crowd. They appear to have been motivated to put something, anything, into the public record, while also making a point of not submitting to the authority of the contest. The desperation of the situation and their consequent recklessness trumped any possible blowback from the embarrassing submission.[17]

Ghost-Writer Called In

This brings us to the last part of the smoke and mirrors. During this time, David Gregory becomes fully engaged in trying to flesh out Newton's cryptic solution. (As we shall see, he became what would be the first in a line of Newton's colleagues who tried to do so.) Previously, in 1696, Gregory had been involved in a project, trying to recast Leibniz's work on the catenary into Newtonian language, but now, sometime before the middle of February, he properly turns to the work of Leibniz's mentor, Christian Huyghens, to pull together a draft on the cycloid. However, he is unable to figure out any way that Newton's vaunted "fluxional" equations do anything to help.

Gregory then meets with Newton on the problem. He made notes on the subsequent meeting, dated March 7th, and they seem to reflect an awkward incapacity on Newton's part to explain much of anything.[18] Finally, on March 17th, evidently after Newton's submission had already been sent off to Bernoulli, Gregory presents to the Royal Society his improved draft on the cycloid. That version was also published in the monthly of the *Philosophical Transactions*, though anonymously. The Newtonian faction would make a feeble effort to pass it off as Newton's second version; the not-so-naked version—but two years later, Wallis had to admit to Leibniz that Newton had not authored it. It was David Gregory.

The Initial Response of Leibniz and Bernoulli

So, neither Newton nor Montague officially recognize the *Acta* contest. They have published, prior to the deadline, their non-solution, and then they arrange for it to be transmitted to Bernoulli via their intermediary, Basnage de Beauval.[19] In late March, in time for the Easter deadline, Basnage sends it to Bernoulli, calling it the "anonymous English solution." On March 30th, Bernoulli writes back to Basnage, pointing out how there is little or nothing there—that the author has concealed his method, if he had one—and that this is unfortunate as the puzzle lies at the frontier of pushing sci-

---

15. Whiteside, D. T. *The Mathematical Papers of Isaac Newton*, Vol. 8, 1981a, p. 74/5. Whiteside himself notes this curious situation.

16. From Newton's "Praxis" manuscript kept at Babson College—and heroically acted out by Peter O'Toole in the movie, "The Ruling Class"!

17. Is this not the state of mind of such as the former head of the CIA, John Brennan, who, when caught in a lie, simply announces that he doesn't do evidence?

18. This author has not seen Gregory's notes; however, after Newton's latter-day defenders examine them, they offer the succinct account: "Either Gregory did not understand Newton's argument, or Newton's explanation was very brief." One can only imagine.

19. Basnage was an advocate in Rotterdam of John Locke. (Locke had been in the Netherlands for most of the 1680's, attendant there to the future King of England, William, prior to the 1688/9 invasion of England.) Otherwise, Basnage was made a member of the Royal Society in 1697, the same time as his role in aiding Montague, the President of the Royal Society.

ence forward. "I would only wish that Mr. Newton had done as we have, that is to say, that he had also published the method that had led him to the discovery of the sought after curve; because that is the way the public gains."

Dealing With Those 'Accustomed to Show Off'

Bernoulli then gives Basnage an example of what he means by acting for the public benefit: He had a more "mathematically-acceptable" solution, but was going to submit and publish his other solution, a concept-driven analysis of light and gravity. "Mr. Leibniz himself told me to do" as such, wrote Bernoulli, as there would be more public benefit. Then his suggestion to Newton: Bernoulli's light-gravity solution, as "simple as it is," is still "of great consequence, and could nicely serve those who are accustomed to show off at the expense of others, as a means of making some little new discoveries, which should be sufficient for them to claim for themselves the possession and all of the glory of the invention." That is Bernoulli's description of Newton's claim to fame, Newton's mathematization of Kepler in *Principia*. Rather, Newton should stop such silly games, for the actual brachistochrone solution is rich enough to help Newton lift himself above his previous habits. Of course, he would have to apply himself to real science.

V. Bernoulli's 'Light-Gravity' Solution

Here ends the chronological account of the nine-month contest. We now present Bernoulli's solution. The May, 1697 *Acta* publishes the six submitted solutions, those by Johann Bernoulli, Leibniz, Jacob Bernoulli, Ehrenfried von Tschirnhaus, the Marquis de l'Hospital, and Newton.[20] Leibniz's historical introduction to the submissions situates the contest in terms of the physical geometry of the transcendental curves, such as the catenary and the brachistochrone (cycloid). He restricts his comments on Newton's submission to the gentle barb: "Newton could solve this problem if he

only undertook the task."

Bernoulli's entry opens with a characterization of what Newton, and others, have done:

> Up to this time so many methods which deal with maxima and minima have appeared that there seems to remain nothing so subtle in connection with this subject that it cannot be penetrated by their discernment—so they think, who pride themselves either as the originators of these methods or as their followers. Now the students may swear by the word of their master as much as they please, and still, if they will only make the effort, they will see that our problem cannot in any way be forced into the narrow confines imposed by their methods, which extend only so far as to determine a maximum or minimum among given quantities....

He then holds up Leibniz as a model for Newton to apply to himself:

> [T]he celebrated Leibniz.... That he would indeed find a solution I had no doubt, for I am sufficiently well acquainted with the genius of this most sagacious man.... The future will show what others will have accomplished. In any case the problem deserves that geometers devote some time to its solution since such a man as Leibniz, so busy with many affairs, thought it not useless to devote his time to it. And it is reward enough for them that, if they solve it, they obtain access to hidden truths which they would otherwise hardly perceive.

Only now does Bernoulli explain his solution. We will present his main conceptual argument, leaving out his subsequent mathematical codification that he showed was a consequence of his method. He begins by bringing up Huyghens' discovery of the tauto-

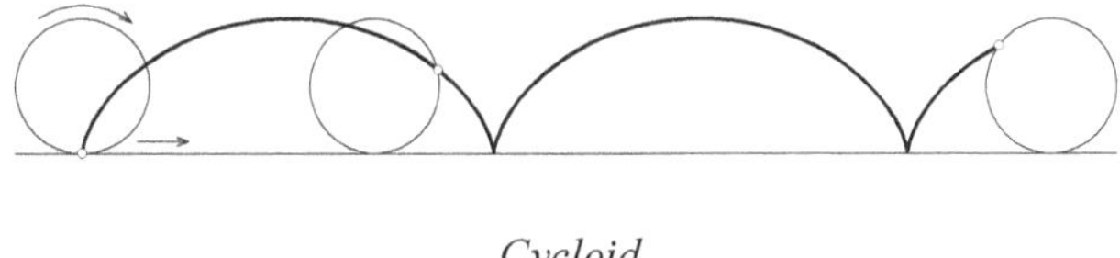

Cycloid

---

20. Tschirnhaus was a longtime collaborator of Leibniz who first published in Leibniz's *Acta* in 1683. L'Hospital was a serious student of Johann Bernoulli and was, twice, the vice-President of the French Academy of Sciences.

chrone ("tauto-chrone" or same time) nature of the cycloid. A cycloid is traced out when one rolls a circular clock one full cycle, whence a given point on the clock, e.g., the "6 o'clock" position, takes a path describing a cycloid.[21] Huyghens had developed the cycloid's curious property that a marble rolling down a cycloidal path reaches the bottom at the same time, regardless of how far up the path it began its descent from. Bernoulli announces: "But you will be petrified with astonishment when I say that precisely this cycloid, the tautochrone of Huygens is our required brachistochrone!" That should get his audience's attention. The cycloid combines within itself, not one, but two seemingly miraculous properties: Every point along the cycloid is, as it were, an equipotential point in a gravitational field, and the cycloid is also the least action pathway, displaying how gravity works.

Light Meets Gravity

Next, Bernoulli announces: "I discovered a wonderful accordance between the curved orbit of a ray of light in a continuously varying medium and our brachistochrone curve." He proceeds to remind the reader of Fermat's principle of least action:

[A] ray of light which passes from a rare into a dense medium [such as from air into water] is bent toward the normal in such a manner that the ray ... traverses the path which is shortest in time. From this principle he shows that the sine of the angle of incidence and the sine of the angle of refraction are directly proportional to the rarities of the media, or to the reciprocals of the densities; that is, in the same ratio as the velocities with which the ray traverses the media. Later the most acute Leibniz in *Act. Erud.*, 1682, p. 185 et. Seq., and soon thereafter the celebrated Huygens in his treatise *de Lumine*, p. 40, proved in detail and justified by the most cogent arguments

---

21. Huyghens had responded to Blaise Pascal's 1658 challenge problems on the cycloid, and studied Pascal's 1659 *Roulettes*. Besides the curiosity of the tautochrone nature of the cycloid, Huyghens' mind found it significant that the cycloid's involute was yet another cycloid, whose evolute was the original cycloid. The singular involute/evolute quality of the cycloid led to Huyghens' unique design of a famous pendulum clock, which could keep time on a rolling ship—crucial for the ship's navigation by the stars.

this same physical or rather metaphysical principle....

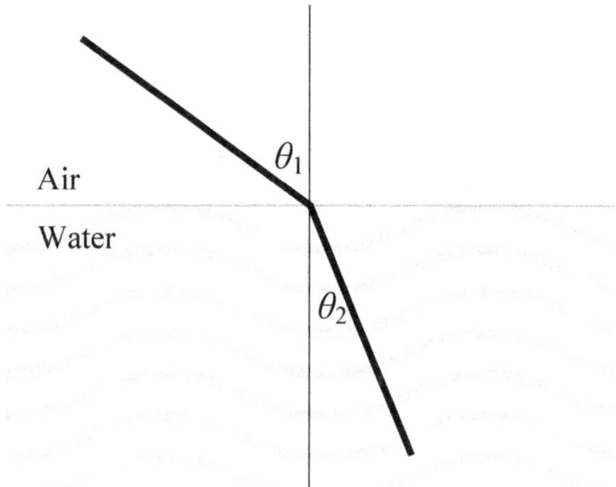

Snell's Sine Law: The proportion of the sines of the two angles gives the proportion of the velocities, or the inverse of the proportion of the densities.

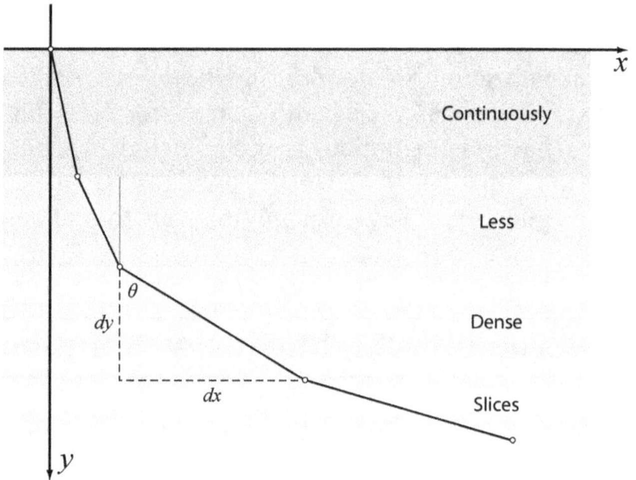

The path of the light ray going through many infinitesimally thin layers, each one less dense than the one above it. Bernoulli develops the direction of the curve from the dx and dy components of each infinitesimal triangle.

One sees a stick partly thrust into water as being bent, and the angle of the bending, or refraction, is related (via the sines of the two angles) to the relative densities of air and water. Bernoulli cites the works of Leibniz and Huyghens that he studied for his development of least action as a solid principle.

Bernoulli then proceeds to generalize Fermat's one layer of refraction by asking the reader to imagine "an infinite number of sheets ... whose interstices are filled with transparent material of rarity … decreasing according to a certain law…." Fermat's one action of refraction will now be applied continuously through each of the infinitely thin layers. Hence, by this construction, the light ray will travel according to the shortest time. And one may choose, in this construction, to have the rarity of the infinitely thin layers be specifically geared to the changes in velocity due to gravity. Hence, the two curves will be the same. The construction is based upon taking the least-action characteristic as primary, even in the smallest incremental steps. So, Bernoulli can conclude:

> For whether the increase in the velocity depends on the nature of the medium… as in the case of the ray of light, or whether one removes the medium, and supposes that the acceleration is produced by means of another agency but according to the same law, as in the case of gravity—since in both cases the curve is in the end supposed to be tra-

versed in the shortest time, what hinders us from substituting the one in place of the other?

Though Fermat had come under attack by mechanists in his day for daring to employ a metaphysical principle such as "least action," Bernoulli showed how, by following this path from Fermat to Huyghens to Leibniz, truly marvelous results were derived—results unimaginable to mere mechanists. Bernoulli, at this point, gives the mathematical bookkeeping for his preceding argument. Then he provides a delightful dessert.

Dessert: The Coup de Grace

Following this tour de force, Bernoulli cannot resist adding a devastating dig at Newton, a coup de grace. Bernoulli admits, completely tongue in cheek, that we've derived the cycloid quite generally, but then adds, as a sort of burlesque, the completely unnecessary and trivial sequel … "We have yet to show how from a given point … we can draw the … cycloid, which passes through a second given point. This is easily accomplished as follows.…" Then, without mentioning Newton's name, he inserts Newton's non-proof, showing how one can enlarge a cycloid! It turns out, Bernoulli shows, there was a use for Newton's demonstration … and, indeed, as stated, it was easy to accomplish the mission of making the cycloid the right size to accommodate the two points A and B. It was ridiculously easy, with emphasis on the ridicule. And that is Bernoulli's point. Bernoulli delivered his coup de grace to the ugly submission, by putting it in its proper place. Recall Figure 1 again.

Of course, for several centuries, commentators on the Brachistochrone Contest have simply missed the joke. At least in Hans Christian Andersen's tale, "The Emperor's New Clothes"—when the little child innocently observes, "But he hasn't got anything on"—everyone's self-deluding behavior is punctured.

VI. Flight Forward: 'By the Claw, the Lion Is Known'

Strap on your seatbelts. The story now goes ballistic. A month after the contest had ended, Basnage publishes the letter that Bernoulli had written to him back on March 30th. There Bernoulli had conveyed to Basnage that it was clear that Newton was the author of the anonymous submission: "We know indubitably that the author is the celebrated Mr. Newton; and, besides, it were enough to understand so by this sample, *ex ungue Leonem*." Bernoulli uses the expression, that from the claw, the lion (is known). From a look at what had been submitted, a lot is known about the person that submitted it. On April 3rd, a few days later, Bernoulli repeats this same formulation in writing to Leibniz. Leibniz had no trouble understanding Bernoulli, writing back, on April 15th, that the Newton submission was indeed "suspicious."

To state the obvious, no normal person would have taken the "claw" comment as a compliment. Rather, Bernoulli had called out Newton in issuing the January 1st leaflet, and he had received the response that the emperor indeed had no clothes on. Newton, the vaunted "Mr. Gravity," could not take the first step in unpacking how gravity works, nor how the calculus could aid in developing such physical investigations. From this simple episode, Bernoulli characterized the whole fraudulent approach of the Newton mathematizing project of the previous ten years.

The World Upside Down

Any reader can try a simple search engine experiment: Put in "Isaac Newton," "lion," and "claw," and you'll get the amazing result that the world has turned upside down. Bernoulli's phrase is universally taken as a great compliment to Newton! (And, of course, you will have to look a lot further to locate anyone who addresses Newton's actual submission.)[22] All you will get is some version of the fantastical claim that Leibniz and Bernoulli thought they could trap Newton, but the genius Newton showed them by his proof that he had the mental strength of a lion, that he was the most powerful thinker in the jungle. Two examples: First is a typical one (by L. T. More from 1931): "It is said that Bernoulli recognized the author from the sheer power and originality of the work…".

---

22. One looks far and wide for even these two modest exceptions: First, in 1810 Robert Woodhouse dismissed Newton's submission with the one-line cryptic comment: Newton "gave, without proof or the authority of his name, a method of describing the cycloid." (The rest of Woodhouse's 1810 "Treatise on Isoperimetrical Problems and the Calculus of Variations" was helpful in bringing a version of Leibniz's analysis back into England, and it served as an impetus for the revival of science in England by John Herschel and Charles Babbage.) Second, Newton's modern-day editor, D. T. Whiteside, amongst his voluminous commentary, slips in the phrase: "Newton's undemonstrated construction of the required curve." Yet, he provides no further elaboration of this point.

Second, Carl Sagan takes flight, in his 2011 *Cosmos*, with: "Before leaving for work the next morning, he had invented an entire new branch of mathematics called the calculus of variations [...and] used it to solve the brachistochrone problem... [T]he brilliance and originality of the work betrayed the identity of its author. When Bernoulli saw the solution, he commented, 'We recognize the lion by his claw.'" Perhaps he should have looked at Newton's submission before he leaped.

We can credit Sir David Brewster as the one who popularized this outrageous take on what Bernoulli wrote. (For Poe's war against Brewster, see p. 53.) Brewster, the British arbiter in the 19th Century for what would be counted as science, was at the core of this lionizing of Newton. His 1855 revised biography of Newton explained that:

> [A]lthough that [submission] of Newton was anonymous, yet Bernoulli recognized in it his powerful mind; 'tanquam', says he, 'ex ungue leonem', as the lion is known by his claw.... When the great geometer of Basle[23] saw the anonymous solution, he recognized the intellectual lion by the grandeur of his claw; and in their future contests on the fluxionary controversy, both he and Leibniz had reason to feel that the sovereign of the forest, though assailed by invisible marksmen, had neither lost a tooth nor broken a claw.[24]

Rather disconcerting—but Sir David Brewster, a student of the intelligence agent John Robison,[25] was in a position to know about Newton's behind-the-scenes activity in the "fluxionary controversy," and it seems

that he took some vicarious pleasure, at the thought of the claw-and-tooth methods Newton would employ to savage Leibniz. Section VIII will cover the assault on Leibniz. First, we clean up the one last part of the story of Newton's submission.

VII. But, Didn't Newton Pick the Correct Multiple-Choice Answer?

Indeed, he did. Newton drew a cycloid, and not the other main suspect, the catenary.

Did this signify anything? Conceivably, but none of Newton's work papers on this contest exist, and there is no indication that Newton had any idea as to how to solve the problem, and every indication that he did not. We shall address the most likely scenario.

Bernoulli had been very clear the previous year that the solution to the challenge contest was a very well-known curve. When it came to rounding up the usual suspects, the catenary and the cycloid were the pre-eminent curves publicly treated by Roberval, Fermat, Pascal, Huyghens, Leibniz and Bernoulli in the previous decades. If one didn't have any other clue and had to back-engineer a solution, one would start with those two suspects. Everyone knows that, on a multiple-choice test, the advantage is that one may not know how to solve the problem, but one can look at the, typically, four possible solutions and work backwards.

No later than the previous summer and fall, two of Newton's collaborators, John Wallis and David Gregory, are known, by a paper trail, to have been working on the contest. They had studied both of the two most likely suspects, and were attempting to, literally, curve-fit them to the required specifications. Though Wallis was fascinated with the cycloid, he wrote to Gregory that, after months of effort, he was stumped.[26] David Gregory rather intelligently went back to the earlier (1691) Catenary Contest proposed by Jakob Bernoulli, where the three solutions were given by the two Bernoulli's and Leibniz.[27] He had pretty good reasons for

___

23. Bernoulli was at Groningen. It was Bernoulli's famous brother Jakob who was the geometer at Basle. Brewster means Johann Bernoulli, who, eight years later, did succeed his brother at Basle.

24. Sir David Brewster's 1855 *Memoirs of the Life, Writings, and Discoveries of Sir Isaac Newton*. Vol. II, page 192.

25. Of note, Sir David Brewster was a student of the Edinburgh intelligence agent, John Robison—the same one who worked so assiduously with his *Proofs of a Conspiracy* to poison the minds of Americans in the 1797/8 period of the Alien and Sedition Acts. The operation to ignore the positive mission of the United States of Washington and Hamilton, and to retreat to a world of choosing up sides—between the British Empire's version of law and order and the Jacobin French reactionary rage—was at the core of the factionalization of the republic of the United States and the cementing into place of turf-protecting political parties.

___

26. Wallis wrote up a history of the cycloid, interestingly tracing it to the work of Nicholas of Cusa, but it is appears that he was stumped as to how to proceed. See Wallis's "Concerning the Cycloid Known to Cardinal Cusanus, about the Year 1450," dated May 4, 1697 and published in the *Philosophical Transactions*.

27. Gregory published in the 1697 *Philosophical Transactions* his unsuccessful attempt to put Leibniz's solution for the catenary into

suspecting that this new 1697 contest would not be a repeat of the catenary.

'Dunned and Teezed by Foreigners'

Perhaps Newton was unaware of the efforts of his colleagues, but it is much more likely that he had been apprized of their efforts, and had also worked over the challenge contest himself. If so, evidently he met with frustration and buried whatever worksheets he had. It would appear that he and the others would have been content to remain silent when the December 31st deadline arrived. However, the extension of the contest until Easter, 1697, and, in particular, the January, 1697 personal delivery of the challenge to Newton's doorstep changed all that. Recall Newton's peevish: "I do not love to be printed upon every occasion much less to be dunned and teezed by foreigners about Mathematical things...."

Hence, it is a decent possibility that the Wallis/Gregory/Newton group's efforts over the preceding half-year enabled them to narrow down the choices to make the cycloid the more likely candidate. Certainly, Gregory had done sufficient work on the catenary that might have convinced him that he had gone down the wrong path.

So, in sum, what we have is, first, that Newton makes the point that he didn't receive the direct challenge until January 29th, meaning that it took an abnormal 38 days after Bernoulli dispatched the challenge for him to see it. Next, Lord Montague, the head of the Royal Society, supposedly receives the solution on January 30th, but the normal reading of such received communications to the weekly Royal Society meetings is missed for the next couple of meetings. Further, their initial actions are not to send in the solution, but to publish, outside of the contest, an anonymous response to be "on the record." And, finally, Gregory works for weeks to produce an improved version, which evidently is not completed soon enough to send in for the contest, but is put into the *Philosophical Transactions*, also anonymously— as if by the same anonymous author of the previous month.

In this world of smoke and mirrors, it is perfectly possible, and eminently likely, that Lord Montague simply decided that Mr. Anonymous would be on record with the cycloid option, and if it worked out, then the association with Newton could be promulgated. But if the wrong multiple-choice selection had been made, deniability as to authorship was fully in play.

VIII. The Assault upon Leibniz

The Montague/Newton faction did not take Bernoulli's advice to stop showing off and begin to learn from the proper solution to the gravity problem (and perhaps even from the gravity of the problem!). They neither investigated the provocative avenue of the coherences between light and gravity nor were they willing to take advantage of Leibnizian analytical techniques. Rather, in the immediate years after the May, 1697 publication of the Brachistochrone solution, there were various attempts to recast the various published solutions into the language of Newtonian fluxions.

A year and a half after the contest had ended, the British Royal Society published a somewhat confused version of Bernoulli's solution, done by one Richard Sault. In 1700, both David Gregory and John Craige worked out their versions of brachistochrone proofs. And in 1704, Craige's version was the model for Charles Hayes' textbook, *A Treatise of Fluxions*, where results from Bernoulli, Leibniz et al, were recast into Newtonian fluxions. But it was the figure closest to Newton, Fatio de Duillier, who worked hardest to extend Newton's mathematics into a proof.[28]

Newton's Favorite Fires the First Shot

Fatio published in 1699 a rather convoluted argument, one which Leibniz found to be "unnecessarily complicated" and "round-about". While his version of a proof was stillborn, bearing no fruitful results, it became infamous for Fatio's flight-forward assault upon Leibniz. He dared to charge Leibniz with being merely a "second inventor" of the calculus—this, just after the power and mastery of Leibniz's calculus had

---

Newtonian fluxions. In 1698, Leibniz pointed out the failure in Gregory's derivation as due to the insufficiency of the fluxions, and suggested Gregory should discuss the matter with Newton. Newton refused.

28. Fatio had a complicated relationship with Newton, one that likely played a role in Newton's psychological breakdown of 1693. Otherwise, Fatio was notorious as a millenialist, one who thought that the world was coming to an end imminently. For Fatio, France's King Louis XIV was the anti-Christ marking such an event.

been publicly displayed, and Newton's publicly humiliated. Today, such a charge by Fatio is taken as received wisdom, a charge that must have some element of truth to it. However, at the time, it was a bolt out of the blue, done by a rather unstable character—but it proved to be the opening shot in the contrived 'Newton-Leibniz' priority dispute that played out from 1699 to 1716, Leibniz's last eighteen years.

The 1696/7 contest had already put an end to any ostensible scientific discussion from the Montague/Newton crowd. Nothing but legalistic and sophistical tricks ensued, degrading into outright fraud. The anti-Leibniz operation went into overdrive in 1711/12, when Leibniz was appointed to key positions in Russia and in the Austro-Hungarian Empire, and had key inroads into the next English government, and English history has never recovered.[29] However, the operation was launched in the wake of the Brachistochrone Contest of 1697.

One might recall that it was Newton himself who, in 1713, wrote the anonymously-issued official report of the British Royal Society and their supposedly neutral investigation by a responsible committee, into the hoked-up debate over who had first invented the calculus. Newton headed the committee and authored the report. It found that Leibniz was wrong and Newton was right. Newton was judge, jury and litigant. If one can prove how gravity works by simply drawing a cycloid, then what is there to stop one from winning all one's arguments by being the anonymous judge of one's own debates?[30]

Such behavior condemned 18th-century England to financial bubbles, to the tax-farming of colonies, and to expanded military deployments—making the American Revolution practically inevitable. The general welfare of a population really does depend upon pushing forward the frontiers of science and developing qualitative breakthroughs in modes of production. To turn one's back on such is to write the date of extinction upon that society.[31]

---

29. This author's account may be found at: https://www.schillerinstitute.org/educ/hist/eiw_this_week/2016/0208-leibnizs_kepler_project.html

30. Or, when eyewitness accounts are brought from Syria to the United Nations to counter blatant lies, isn't the proper behavior for a British imperialist to simply walk out and refuse to hear the testimony?

31. A somewhat ironic point: In 1704, Newton calculated the world would end in 356 years. (Before you go sell the farm, remember, Newton has been known to engage in frauds!)

IX. Are Light and Space Alive?

They sure seem to act that way. Light bends toward the more dense medium so as to minimize the overall time of its action. Substance is so distributed as to structure spatial relations, so that parts act on other parts in a way that we label "gravity."

The implications would await the further developments of Bernhard Riemann and Alfred Einstein; however, for Leibniz and the Bernoullis, the activity of light and the substance of mass were not two fundamentally distinct entities to be understood in their external actions upon each other. That light bends toward (not away from) the more dense medium speaks to a non-negligible substantiality of light. That the topological arrangement of mass has, inescapably, a dynamic potential wrapped up in it (e.g., Leibniz's "vis viva") speaks to a vibrant quality of substantiality. A simplistic world of dead, inert pieces of matter being subjected to collisions with other such, certainly qualifies as a simple world, one amenable to simpler quantification - but not one that ever did or could exist.

Rather, the provocative and sometimes paradoxical aspects of the "self-reflexivity" associated with humans (e.g., looking over one's own shoulder; deliberation; acting based upon an intention; etc.) have a reflection in non-human animal life, in plant life, and even in the so-called inorganic realm of substance. (Or, in Vladimir Vernadsky's terms, the noetic organizes the organic, which organizes the inorganic.) This is what unites a body falling under its own weight, and a light ray refracting through a consistently-varying medium. The body participates in re-structuring the space through which it moves, and the light organizes the medium through which it moves.

How Human Are Light and Space?
Light does not self-consciously deliberate, with an active dialogue in its head, pausing to reflect—as you the reader have been doing. However, it does originate from a sun-powered solar system, and it does travel through a changing medium according to a least-action principle—not because it has an on-board computer doing the calculations, but because activity and substance are fundamentally inter-related; and the conjoined two, as Leibniz explained it, would simply never have a reason to waste time, lolly-gagging. Having no reason to do so, they would go about their mission in a direct, least action fashion.

While light seems to know where it needs to end up, and seems to demonstrate what we would identify as an intention, that appearance involves a confusion rooted in our own mythology of our own self-consciousness and our own intentional activity. The light ray was never really an individual thing standing around waiting for something to do. It was always bound up in a bigger process. Too often we tend to think of ourselves as a "Robinson Crusoe" on the outside of the universe looking in. But it is when a human solves the scientific problem of locating his or her mission in life, locates the reason for having been born, that intention is properly located. And this self-reflexive activity occurs as part and parcel of the individual coming to terms with one's Maker, with one's mortality, and with one's admiration and love for the Creator's creation, including one's fellow man. Indeed, the way human intention plays out is at the core of scientific method. It is not about getting a life counselor and an investment planner, assumedly to manage the time left on the ticking clock.

The family of transcendental curves that Leibniz and his circle developed in the early 1690's originated from such considerations. The catenary—a chain suspended at each end and pulled upon by gravity—has a specific shape, unique to the mapping of one's location within a topological distribution of substances. Its shape is as unique as its location in space! The tautochrone displays equipotential pathways through non-empty space. The brachistochrone, or least-time curve, speaks to how action occurs—as Bernoulli emphasized, be it gravitational or the energetic of light transmission. And the golden-mean spiral[32] is a hallmark of a world created, whereby the creations are a lawful reflection of the Creator—where man is made in the image of God. So, light did not *have* to refract toward substance, and creations did not *have* to be made in the image of their

A ball rolling down the pictured cycloid curve will always arrive at the bottom before a ball rolling down a straight path.

Creator—but that would not have been good. And God is good.

X. If God Is Good, Why Do Lies Last So Long?

Abraham Lincoln famously declared that one can fool some of the people all the time, and all of the people some of the time, but one cannot fool all the people all the time. He wasn't making a point about polls or numbers. The point is that there is indeed a reality principle, where, below the level of most people's perception, certain things have to be successfully accomplished, lest no one is around to debate the point. There is no world where all the people have been fooled all the time.

For his inauguration in March, 1865, Abraham Lincoln chose to address Americans—as victory was in their grasp after four years of bloody insurrection—not on how much they had sacrificed and accomplished, but how they must come to a better understanding of their Creator. There would come moments when they would wonder what it was all about, and whether it was worth it, and why a good God would put them through all that suffering. However, they must not allow into their hearts the notion that God was uncaring or mean. For the violence of the war to not continue its destruction into peacetime, the population had to become unprecedentedly better people.

Lincoln put to his audience that, if it were not four years of blood to pay the debt, but two-hundred and fifty, then that was the measure of what it took to expiate the sin of slavery; and that God knew a type

---

32. In brief, the simpler golden section is the specific action (sectioning) that divides a length so that the larger portion to the smaller portion is in the same relationship as the whole length was to the larger portion. As such, the characteristic action embeds the whole-to-part relationship into the larger-part-to-smaller-part relationship. The relationship of the created parts reflects the way the Creator went about creating. Study of that relationship brings one closer to the Creator.

of measurement that was of a higher species than most other measuring, and formation of judgments, that people do. The suggestion was that people should struggle to get inside the Creator's mind and change themselves in a way that would otherwise have been deemed impossible. Stay the same, and your loved ones would have died in vain. It was a hard speech.

British Empire Lies Today

With the world on the verge of growing up, of maturing beyond "dog-eat-dog" geopolitical scheming, the type of lying coming out of imperial ideologues may worry people, it may anger or even enrage people, but it is a stage of lying and bluster of a cornered beast. Since China has recently committed to taking the lead in ending geopolitical gamesmanship and to offering countries long-term and infrastructure-driven development, the lying and blustering political habits of the recent fifty years, have been undercut. The Wizard of Oz really is rather pathetic.

The only problem with three centuries of obsessive blindness as to what Newton did is that our civilization has been too scared to laugh. The fellow really did commit an outrageous piece of buffoonery. If the Creator has allowed obsessive blocking on the joyful capacity of creative mentation to linger for three centuries, then the Creator also allowed for healthy laughter to relax humans and allow them to move forward—to move forward as a transformed population, one having formed a long-overdue, passionate and sustained commitment to wipe out poverty, hunger and disease, and to bring the genius out of every precious newborn.

Newton's buffoonery, or the desperation today of the likes of MI6's Richard Dearlove, are jokes in God's universe. While one should not be needlessly cruel to the pathetic, still it would be worse than impolite not to laugh at God's jokes. God tells jokes for a reason. And since it is vital that we don't waste the evils of the past by a failure to transform ourselves appropriately today, some healthy humor, in recognition of what we will never submit to again, is therapeutic and probably necessary.

Edgar Allan Poe's War Against Brewster: No More Creeping and Crawling

Sir David Brewster was the chief promoter of Isaac Newton in the first half of the 19th Century and the main public figure for the British Empire's posture on science. Edgar Allan Poe, the American poet, used Brewster's posturings to push Americans toward a powerful conception of science and of mind. Here, we (1) reveal Brewster's method in terms of his attempted defense of Newton's sanity; (2) compare Brewster's sophistries with Newton's actual words; and then (3) show Poe's exposure of this method in his essay, "Maelzel's Chess Player."

I. Brewster's Humbuggery

Newton's ridiculous submission in the 1697 brachistochrone contest was recognized by Johann Bernoulli, the designer of the contest, as symptomatic of something very wrong with Newton's whole approach to actual science. Newton's submission was done anonymously, but Bernoulli employed the phrase "from the claw, the lion is known" to encapsulate the bizarre submission. Sir David Brewster's 1831 biography of Newton is the prime source for the bizarre interpretation, whereby Bernoulli's apt characterization actually meant that Bernoulli had been overwhelmed by the power and genius of Newton's submission.

The larger context of Brewster's biography was perhaps equally bizarre. It opens with his announcement that it was his "sacred duty" to both England and Christianity to defend Newton.

Brewster had been provoked by an inclusion of a 1694 report by Huyghens (printed in 1822 biography of Newton by the French scientist, Biot) that Newton had endured a period of insanity but fortunately was in recovery.[1] Though this had been known at the time by

---

1. Huyghens: "On the 29th May, 1694, M. Colin, a Scotsman, informed me that eighteen months ago the illustrious geometer, Isaac Newton, had become insane... When he came to the Archbishop of Cambridge, he made some observations which indicated an alienation of mind." He has "so far recovered his health that he began to understand the Principia." (The Archbishop was John Tillotson, husband of Cromwell's

Lord Montague and John Locke and others of Newton's circle, Brewster pretends that no one in England ever had even a clue that Newton suffered such a malady.[2] He claimed that he would present the true story of "that temporary indisposition which, from the view that has been taken of it by foreign philosophers, has been the occasion of such deep distress to the friends of science and religion."

What Brewster meant by such is that he accepted the patronage of one Lord Braybrooke to go public with components of the private "Newton" file, attempting to put a different spin on the recently-surfaced Huyghens' report.[3] For that purpose, Braybrooke gave Brewster access to the pertinent correspondence of Newton, John Locke, and Samuel Pepys, kept in reserve all these years. Brewster argued that Huyghens must be wrong because Brewster can cite parts of the eighteen-month period prior to Huyghens' May 29, 1694 report, where Newton appears sane. However, in his concern to present examples of sanity, Brewster includes incidents a year earlier than what Huyghens reported, and uses that to show that Huyghens could not have been right. Further, the evidence he does present only multiplies the confusion as it is of varying degrees of relevancy and accuracy. His method seems to be one of wearing down the opposition.

II. The Facts in the Case of Newton's 'Alienation of Mind'

Simply compare what Huyghens related (see footnote 1) with what Brewster submitted from Newton's

Sir David Brewster

previously-unknown letters from 1693. Here are two examples. Newton lashed out against Samuel Pepys, the Secretary to the Admiralty, who had worked to reward Newton with a post in the new government: "…[F]or I am extremely troubled at the embroilment I am in, and have neither ate nor slept well this twelvemonth, nor have my former consistency of mind. I never designed to get anything by your interest, nor by King James's favour, but am now sensible that I must withdraw from your acquaintance, and see neither you nor the rest of my friends any more.…" Huyghens had indicated November, 1692, as the approximate date of Newton's mental problems; Newton, in September, 1693, references a difficult "twelvemonth" period—roughly a variance of two months in the time of onset.

To John Locke, the man who would eventually succeed in arranging for Newton's post at the Royal Mint, Newton wrote: "Being of opinion that you endeavoured to embroil me with women, and by other means, I was so much affected with it, as that when one told me you were sickly and would not live, I answered, 'twere better if you were dead." This, from mid-September 1693, was just after Newton had begun to recover.

So, there is little doubt that, from the winter of 1692 until September 1693, Newton suffered his difficulties, climaxing in August and early September. Without attempting to explain Newton's dismay over embroilments with women, it seems that one contributing factor was Newton's anxiety over an appointment from the King. Brewster both produced the letters and failed to impugn Newton's testimony! Regardless, Brewster is able to summarize: "In reviewing the details which we have given … from the beginning of 1692 till 1695, it is impossible to draw any other conclusion than that he possessed a sound mind."

Such humbuggery—or to use Poe's word, cant—was little to Poe's liking.

---

niece and politically very close to Lord and Lady Russell, through whom, he became closely tied to the new rulers, William and Mary.)

2. Brewster: "…[T]his incident has been for more than a century unknown to his own countrymen, and has been accidentally brought to light by the examination of the manuscripts of Huygens."

3. Lord Braybrooke was the grandson of both Prime Minister George Grenville and General Charles Cornwallis. Grenville authored the infamous Stamp Act. After the "world turned upside down" on Cornwallis at Yorktown, Virginia in 1781, he extracted revenge as Military Governor in India and then Ireland.

III. Poe's Exposure of Brewster's Method

Edgar Allan Poe not only was brilliant at taking the air out of the sails of the British Empire's epistemological frauds, but he exploited the frauds so as to make Americans better. The frauds were aimed at the weaknesses and undeveloped aspects of American culture; hence, they were efficient instruments for confronting Americans on matters of continued mental subservience to the British Empire, long after the Revolutionary War had been won.

Edgar Allan Poe

Memorable is Poe's satirical treatment of both the deductive method of Aries Tottle and his "greatest disciples... one Nueclid and one Can't," and the inductive method of "one Hog," or Francis Bacon, whose scheme was tied "altogether to Sensation... The savants now maintained that the Aristotelean and Baconian roads were the sole possible avenues to knowledge... two preposterous paths—the one of creeping and the one of crawling—which they have dared to confine the Soul that loves nothing so well as to soar..."[4] At the center of the deductive/inductive ideology was the British Association for the Advancement of Science, headed by Sir David Brewster.

Poe's 1836 essay, "Maelzel's Chess Player,"[5] took on Brewster's method, one whose appeal to commonsensical matters primarily dulled the senses as to reality. Poe had read Brewster's 1835 *Letters on Natural Magic*, where Brewster had promulgated a non-solution of the puzzle of a chess automaton, judging it to be a "thorough and satisfactory explanation." As in the brachistochrone contest, the answer was correct, though it was based on fallacious reasoning. Poe wrote that it suffered from "a course of reasoning exceedingly unphilosophical," though it "has contrived to blunder upon a plausible solution."

In brief, audiences in Europe and America had been challenged by the puzzle of what appeared to be a chess-playing machine. Brewster's "thorough and satisfactory explanation" simply showed a way that a human could have been hidden inside the machine. Plenty of diagrams were provided as to what panel could slide where and in what order. Poe agreed that a human was, indeed, inside the apparatus, but seized upon Brewster's humbuggery—the conceit, that showing one of many possible sequences of mechanical manipulations to hide a human in the apparatus, constituted a proof. Rather, for Poe, it was merely a demonstration of the possibility of doing so. Poe proceeded to display an actual solution by relentlessly honing in on the subtle but distinctively human characteristics that could be detected in the operation of the chess automaton.[6] Poe would do no differently with today's proponents of artificial intelligence who are confused that machines somehow will replace the human mind.

Poe's treatment of Brewster's problem with the chess-automaton problem mirrored Brewster's problem with Newton's breakdown. And even though Brewster was never quite as ridiculous as Newton's submission, Poe's treatment of Brewster also reflected Bernoulli's treatment of Newton.[7] By the claw of Brewster's treatment of the case of Newton's mental wonderings, one may know the method of British cultural warfare against science.

---

4. "Mellonta Tauta" was published in 1849, Poe's last year.

5. J. N. Maelzel, the designer of the metronome and of a hearing apparatus for Beethoven, toured the United States in 1825 with his chess automaton, one designed by Wolfgang von Kempelen. Poe witnessed the display several times.

6. The best, and more complete, account of this matter is to be found in "Edgar Allan Poe: The Lost Soul of America" by the Poe expert, Allen Salisbury. "Fidelio", Vol. XV, 2006. http://schillerinstitute.org/fid_02-06/2006/061_-2_Poe_Allen-S.html

7. Much more could be said about Poe's grasp of epistemology and science. Here, merely note: Poe promoted the first American biography of Gottfried Leibniz; and he also praised, with considerable insight, the project to finally publish the complete works of Johannes Kepler—especially since a "singular fatality seems, indeed, not only to have accompanied that wonderful man through life, but to have attached itself even to his works after death."

IV. LaRouche's Foresight

JULY 18, 1999

Can You, Personally, Survive This Bust?

by Lyndon H. LaRouche, Jr.

The head of the Bank of England, Eddie George, has been caught running a theft-ring, stealing what is now approaching $1 billion, or possibly even more, from his own bank. That fact, in itself, should warn you, that Eddie George must be expecting the world financial system, and your personal mutual fund account, to blow out and melt down very soon. If that is not enough to awaken you credit-card slaves from your dreaming, try the next set of facts about Eddie's gold scam.

Eddie's scam involved setting up a special, private market, for letting only certain cronies in on this raid on the Bank of England's gold reserves.[1] Tons of outsiders were eager to buy the gold at those prices, but were kept out. So much for Britain's "free market" policies. Eddie's cronies included some among the same batch of scavengers who were named in an earlier scam, the 1998 U.S. Federal Reserve bail-out of Long Term Capital Management (LTCM), as financial backers of professed "playing-field leveller" Vice-President Al Gore.[2]

But, that is not the end of the story. It becomes much

Eddie George makes a withdrawal from his own bank.

worse. Leading bankers directing divisions of many of the world's biggest banks, are running world-wide scams, looting their own banks, in operations totalling to amounts nearly as big and bad, or worse than Eddie's pilfering of Bank of England gold reserves. Before these current, globalized swindles come to an end, it will be the taxpayers—including the U.S. taxpayers and ordinary bank depositors, who will have been cheated by the Bank of England and its Wall Street accomplices.

One of the toughest questions for honest accoun-

---

1. What Eddie has done, is to sell the Bank of England's gold to his accomplices, at prices far below its value. The take on the margin of difference, runs into the equivalent of billions of U.S. dollars. See Richard Freeman and John Hoefle, "Eddie George's Strategy to Steal the Gold," in this *Feature*.

2. On the LTCM bail-out, and on the roster of carrion-crows working with Eddie George to loot the Bank of England's gold reserves, see John Hoefle, "Global Reverse-Leverage Collapse Is Underway," *EIR*, Oct. 23, 1998.

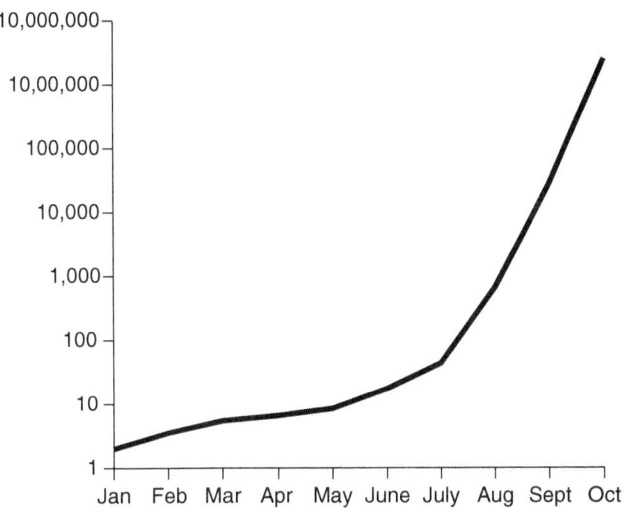

Source: *Zahlen zur Geldentwertung in Deutschland 1914 bis 1923.*

tants to answer, today, is, which, if any, among the world's leading banks might be, just possibly, actually solvent, among virtually all the others, which are not. For reasons which I shall point out to you in a few moments, the facts show, with absolute certainty, that the world's financial system, taken as a whole, is hopelessly bankrupt.

Against less than an estimated $12 trillions-equivalent, and falling rapidly, of world trade as a whole, the largest component of world debt is not less than a still-zooming, estimated $300 trillions-equivalent of short-term pure speculation, known as either "financial derivatives," or related kinds of financial trash-paper.

This derivatives bubble is currently expanding at a rate of not less than 70% per year, the rate of expansion currently necessary to keep the bubble from collapsing into the biggest financial crash in history. By early autumn, the rate of growth of that bubble needed to keep it from imploding, if it had not already crashed, would be skyrocketting far above the 70%-per-year rate, and still climbing like a rocket. The present situation in the world's financial system is comparable to the explosion of German Reichsmark hyperinflation, during the Summer and early Autumn of 1923. [**Figure 1.**]

Given the ratio of rate of growth, of hundreds of tril-

lions dollar-equivalent of financial debt, to a few tens of trillions-equivalent real assets, world wide, and given the rate of skyrocketting of financial debt to presently collapsing assets against such debt-claims, the world's present financial system, the so-called International Monetary Fund (IMF) system, banks and all, is hopelessly bankrupt. Is that IMF, therefore, the same "proven expert" to which nations must turn, in utmost obedience, for advice?

So the story goes, on and on. Today, thoughtful leading bankers themselves are not certain as to which, if any, of the leading individual banks of the Americas or western Europe, if any, might actually be relative exceptions to the general rule. One of the big accounting problems, today, is the fact that, because of continuing deregulation mania within much of the U.S. Congress, and within relevant other agencies, no one knows how many tens of trillions of dollars-worth, or more, of unreported, off-balance-sheet derivatives and related debt, in addition to the estimated $300 trillions figure, are actually hanging out there.

I can report, from personal experience over decades, that the basic principle in all of these scams, underlies the same methods used by professional swindlers in the case of numbers of the cases which I was involved in investigating, in both the U.S.A. and Canada, back during the 1950s, and later. This is the same kind of swindle, looting your own firm, through the magic tricks used, in former times, to run bunco operations through revolving doors in bankruptcy and probate scams.[3] The difference is, these present, giant scams are

---

3. To get the idea of how this works, take the following two stories as typical of the principle involved in such swindles.

In the first case, banker "A" makes a loan to client "B." "B" uses the proceeds of the loan, to cover delivery of merchandise, on credit, to customer "C." Customer "C," in turn, delivers goods, "under the counter," to a retailer, "D." "D" sells these at below average-retail ("discount"), mixed with sale goods for which "D" actually purchased and paid "C" and other manufacturers. "C" falls into bankruptcy; the bank loses; "D" runs off with the skim. Remember the famous "Salad Oil Swindle"? (Norman C. Miller, *The Great Salad Oil Swindle* [New York: Coward McCann, 1965]). As in arson as insurance fraud, there is collusion; there is theft at the expense of looted financial institutions. The second case is a legendary story from U.S. World War II days. A man employed in a high-security war-production plant came out of the plant, at his quitting-time, punctually each day. Each day, he was pushing a wheelbarrow full of sand. The diligent plant guards, becoming more curious with each passing day, searched through the sand with increasing zeal, looking for some valuable object concealed with the sand. After the war, one of the guards met the former wheelbarrow pusher at a local bar.

"Come on, Joe," the guard said; "What were you stealing?"

being run under the cover of the "globalization" hoax, scams run from inside the world's biggest banking and financial houses, this time on a "globalized" scale.

There is only one condition under which so many among the world's leading bankers and private financial houses would, or could collaborate in running such schemes that openly, on that kind of scale. It occurs only when those swindlers are panicked by their knowledge, that the system is about to melt down; they are getting out with as much as they can, while the getting is still good. At this stage, it is only the proverbial poor suckers who are still duped into deluding themselves with the belief that they are "riding out the coming lucky correction." Most of these bankers and leading financial houses are trying, desperately, to keep the public from facing the reality of the situation. Most among the swindlers who are denying the fact of the onrushing crash, are up to their lips in the same kind of financial sewage which they pretend, with their show of Nashville-Agrarian-style "genteel refinement," does not exist.[4]

The most important fact to be learned from Eddie George's scam, is that, in any situation resembling the quality of international crises now piling up, the issues of raw political power soon overwhelm, and replace all ordinary kinds of finance and politics. That kind of period in history, which the present financial crisis reflects, has always been a time during which the greatest political, military, and related upheavals have tended to erupt with suddenness, and with the greatest violence. As we approach the end of this calendar year, any attempt to continue what has passed for "politics as usual" during the recent decades, is about to be blown violently from the world map of the decade or more immediately ahead.

In modern European history, such periods of crisis have always been foreseen among some of the influential people of those times, but, with rare exceptions, nations and their leaders have stubbornly refused to face clearly foreseeable consequences, until after those consequences exploded in their faces. Populations, and most of their leaders, cling to doomed old ways, even after global storms of extreme and protracted violence have begun to sweep the old world order from the po-

litical map. So, Europe was plunged into the follies of World Wars I and II, and into that Great Depression of the 1930s, which less foolish men foresaw, even before the ink was dried on the Treaty of Versailles, as "the economic consequences of the peace."[5]

We can not afford to repeat those kinds of mistakes again; unfortunately, at the present moment, the U.S. establishment, like the governments and others in western Europe, seems to have a suicidal obsession, either out of raw political fear, or delusions, for clinging to the old ways which now threaten to wipe both today's institutions and popular delusions from the map of world history. We might hope that the governments themselves would act to both change those institutions and rid themselves of those delusions, before it is too late.

It is possible, that you and your neighbors might, personally, survive the epoch-shattering crisis now rushing down upon us all. The question is not, "Whether my money can survive?" The question is, "Will you and your family survive?"

In other words, that means, "Will I, my family, and our government, come out of this mess with the political power needed to create the needed *new money-system*, to replace the hopelessly bankrupt old one, the instant the crash of the present world system occurs?" People who ask the latter question, are sane; those who ask, "Then, where do I invest my money?" are probably not sane—at least, not at the present moment; we hope their mental health might be improved by aid of what I report here.

There are three things which you must know, if you are going to qualify as a potential survivor:

1. Why the global financial crash is now inevitable, and soon. Why the world is now overripe for the biggest bust in history, about now.

2. How you and the United States economy might survive the crash.

3. You must recognize and reject those popular delusions, those which have caused nearly all of you to continue to be fooled into acting as if you were political supporters of that mass financial lunacy which allowed this collapse of the system to become inevitable.

<hr>

Joe grinned. After a pregnant pause, he replied: "Wheelbarrows." Joe was using the same Plotto-scheme principle typically used by even the high and mighty. It is an old gag, but it continues to be used by swindlers of all shapes and sizes, like Eddie George today.

4. Like the Count Ugolino of Dante Alighieri's *Inferno*.

5. John Maynard Keynes, *The Economic Consequences of the Peace* (New York: Harcourt, Brace and Howe, 1920).

1. Why the Crash Is Inevitable

Ask yourself, "Why is this crash inevitable?" There are two parts to the answer to that question.

First, in theory, an *uncontrolled crash* might have been prevented—last September-October, for example, if the President of the U.S.A., acting in cooperation with a significant number of other perfectly sovereign nation-states, were to have put the present international financial and monetary system, suddenly, into government-controlled bankruptcy reorganization. In that case, an uncontrolled form of world-wide "crash" could have been prevented. In practice, so far, no prospective head of state of the U.S.A. or western Europe, except for this Democratic Presidential pre-candidate, has the combined inclination, knowledge, and guts to do such a thing; and, I am not President—at least, not yet.

Therefore, if President Clinton does not act as I would have acted, soon, it is the big, chaotic panic of a bust which we must look forward to, soon. As long as that is the case, a wildly uncontrolled global financial crash, is inevitable for the near future. Whether before New Year's Day 2000, or not, is still in doubt. Either way, controlled or uncontrolled, the crash will occur soon, and, among other things, it will bankrupt every greedy sucker who feared that he might get out of the market "too soon." Many among the big names, like Eddie George's cronies, are in the process of bailing out, now.

For the second part of that answer: under the condition I have just described, the crash is inevitable, because there is no way in which the present global financial system could continue to exist, except under the kind of government-supervised bankruptcy-reorganization I had wished President Clinton might have launched last September. With nothing better than that one, only existing real alternative available, the world's present financial system is hopelessly bankrupt. Nothing could save it. We could save the world's economies, but we could not save neither the present world financial system, nor the present monetary system. Only fools would attempt to bail out either of the latter two institutions.

The Crash Is Already On

That financial crash of which we are speaking, is already here.

Up to this moment of writing, there have been many recent crashes, including that of June 10-11, 1999. The new period of global financial collapse, which began with the outbreak of the Brazil crisis (which fools claim that George Soros helped to prevent), never stopped. It has taken the form of a series of increasingly frequent financial crises.

So far, overall, the new round of collapse of the world financial system which erupted in February 1999, has not yet assumed the form which people commonly associate with their more or less distorted image of the 1929 stock-market crash. Nonetheless, the real crash is already here. It has been here since February 1999.

Up to the present moment of writing, the February-July phase of the ongoing blow-out, has taken the following form. Imagine that you are walking across what you had thought to have been solid ground. Then, you experience an eerie feeling, as the ground around you seems to turn soft and wobbly, as you might expect from past experiences of earthquakes. Gradually, what you had thought was solid ground, seems to turn into quicksand. It becomes more and more dangerous. That is another form of a generalized financial crash, one of the worst kinds.

Soon, that will change. At some point soon, you will recognize that we have reached a condition comparable to the verge of the Autumn 1923 disintegration of the Weimar Germany Reichsmark. When that comes, it is more likely to erupt in a form recognizable as more of a "nuclear-style meltdown," than the so-called "1929 style" of crash.

The reason for the present weeks quicksand effect, is that every leading institution of relevance is in a very special kind of "crisis management" mode. As Eddie George's looting of the Bank of England typifies the situation, these institutions are dumping financial and other assets left and right, even at fire-sale prices, turning every financial asset, if possible, into either hard assets, or as much cash as they can squirrel away for the day after the collapse of the entire system has touched bottom.

At the same time, the same institutions are lying wildly, promising that there will never be an actual crash. That is being said just to keep the proverbial suckers—such as mutual funds investors, and duped members of the U.S. Congress—quiet.

This combined effort, by the so-called crisis managers, to squirrel away cash and hard-commodity assets, is in the process of producing an effect comparable to what happened in the Summer phase of the 1923 Weimar Germany Reichsmark hyperinflation. The attempt to maintain squirreled monetary assets, is at the point of generating a hyperinflation in hard commodity assets, like the Summer and Fall of 1923 Germany. [**Figure 2.**]

Germany and Hyperinflation, 1921-23

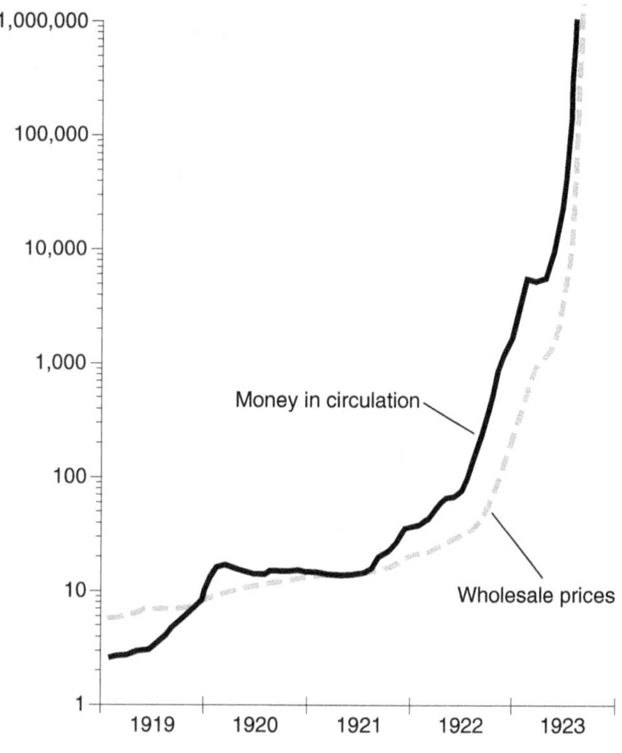

Source: Knut Borchardt, "Wachstum und Wechsellagen 1914-1970," in Hermann Aubin and Wolfgang Zorn (eds.), *Handbuch der deutschen Wirtschafts- und Sozialgeschichte,* Stuttgart: Klett, 1976, vol. 2, p. 699.

What is happening world-wide, as of this moment, is that the relevant institutions are locked into that increasingly frantic sort of crisis-management mode, which has itself become the cause for the new phase of the ongoing quicksand-style crash. Crucial is the frantic traffic launched in the effort to prevent what is called "the Yen carry trade" from blowing out the system in a thermonuclear implosion. That effort to "crisis-manage" the Yen carry-trade bubble, has been transformed from what had been foolishly believed to have been an at least temporary solution, into the new form of the crisis. The crisis-management "medicine" has become a more terrible danger than the disease whose effects it was supposed to control. [See box.]

Given, that terrifying present situation, the good news is, that government would be capable of protecting, intact, the pensions and modestly sized savings of ordinary people, and will keep needed local banks operating, even if those banks are hopelessly bankrupt, and kept alive only as needed social institutions of localities, under government-directed bankruptcy reorganization.

The good news is, also, that the power of the U.S. Federal Government, acting under the "general welfare clause" which is the fundamental law of our Constitution, is the basis for preventing waves of foreclosures on residential housing and similar situations. Apart from those actions, every other financial claim will either be wiped off the books (at least $300 trillions worth world-wide), "frozen," or subject to a schedule of renegotiations.

It is past time that each of you faced up to that reality. Get out of the dream-world, and into the real world. Do it now.

Later, here, I shall identify the delusions of every fool who thinks that the world's financial system is "a zero-sum game." Anyone who believes that financial crashes occur because "some people talk us into it," are not economists; they are mental-health cases, and definitely not healthy ones. That discussion comes later in this report, under the heading of psychological factors responsible for the financial crash. That said, now look at the facts about the crash itself.

How This Collapse Was Organized

Since approximately 1966-1967, the world economy under the International Monetary Fund, has been following a three-pronged track, just as I have described this by my now world-famous "Triple Curve." [**Figure 3**].

The top curve shows a running average of trends in growth, a hyperbolic curve now zooming into the steepest part of its upward slope. That, the approaching world-wide financial crash, is the big financial "balloon note," whose growth has been sending the Dow-Jones skyrocketting over the broad sweep of the 1988-1999 period to date.

The upward curve just below that, not as steep as the financial curve, describes the trend in expansion of money supply. This trend has been dominant since the aftermath of that Trilateral Commission/New York Council on Foreign Relations program, called "controlled disintegration of the economy," which was introduced by Federal Reserve Chairman Paul A. Volcker, over the interval 1979-1982.

It is the type of measures introduced since the enacting of the wildly insane Garn-St Germain and Kemp-Roth laws, which have caused a cancerously growing

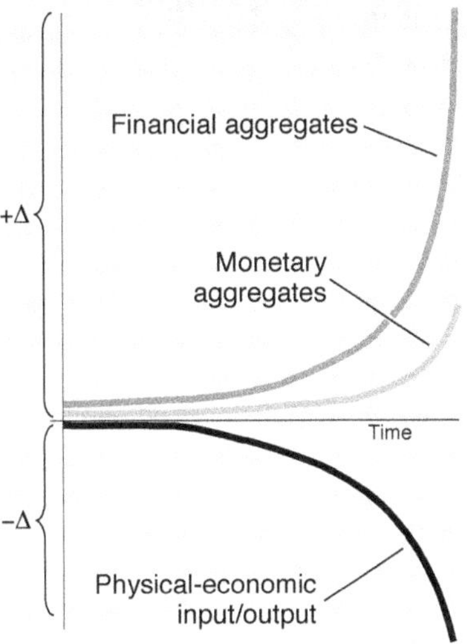

financial bubble, which, in cahoots with the Federal Reserve System, have propelled a self-feeding rate of expansion of the money-supply.

To see the result of that, look at the way the pattern of deregulation measures since Garn-St Germain and Kemp-Roth, has fed an increasingly highly-leveraged growth of this vast, ever-blooming financial bubble. This bubble is a copy, in principle, of the famous Tulip bubble of the Seventeenth Century, and the two John Law-style bubbles which bankrupted much of France and England during the early Eighteenth Century. It is similar to the debt-bubble which plunged mid-Fourteenth-Century Europe into a prolonged "new dark age." The difference is, that the present bubble is global, and more deadly than any other financial bubble known in earlier world history.[6]

Next, look at the bottom of the three curves, the one curving downward: *the long-term trend in decline of real physical-economic incomes and outputs of the U.S. economy, since 1966-1967.*

The measures of deregulation of basic economic infrastructure, banking, transportation, and agriculture, which the Trilateral Commission introduced through the Carter Administration, in 1977-1981, were followed by that savage sort of Wall Street-directed financial deregulation, a legalized scam which has continued to follow the pattern set by Garn-St German and Kemp-

Roth. These combined measures of Carter Administration and post-Carter deregulation, have been reenforced in their effects, by a continued acceleration of the "post-industrial" utopian program launched globally in 1972.[7]

The spread of the policy of "post-industrial" utopianism, which the Carter Administration unleashed in full inside the U.S.A., has gutted our nation's maintenance of its basic economic infrastructure, agriculture, and industry, replacing that production of real wealth upon which continued human existence depends, by the inedible economic hot air of "services" and "information."

The Carter Administration's Trilateral deregulation program, followed by the Republican drive for Garn-St Germain and Kemp-Roth models of financial deregulation, set the trend for the process of step-by-step disintegration of the U.S. real economy. This disintegration has continued to unfold, and accelerate, during the entire 1977-1999 period to date.

Now focus attention upon the bottom of the three curves. The downturn represented by this curve, reflects the way in which the growth of the monetary and financial bubbles has accelerated the per-capita collapse of net real national income and physical net output of the U.S.A., over the course of the 1966-1999 period to date. [**Figures 4-7.**] A similar pattern has been seen throughout all of the Americas, in Africa, and in western Europe and Japan, during most of the same two-plus decades as a whole. [See "Triple Curve" article.]

This third, downward curve, draws attention to the most important side of today's real economic problem. Follow my description of how this side of the process has worked. After that is clear, return to the relationship among the three curves considered as a single physical-economic function.

The Bush Leaguers Raped Our Economy

The current, skyrocketting rates of mergers and acquisitions, globally, reflects a continuing trend of economic cannibalism, launched by Garn-St Germain and Kemp-Roth, through "junk bonds" and related measures, over the entire 1982-1999 interval to date.

---

6. For that reason, our financial and monetary officials are rightly identified today as "bubblers."

7. Canadian oligarch Maurice Strong launched the program as General Secretary of the 1972 Stockholm conference on the environment, where he warned about the alleged onset of global warming, the devastation of forests, the loss of biodiversity, the polluted oceans, and the population explosion. See, Scott Thompson, "Maurice Strong Discusses His Pal Al Gore's Dark Age 'Cloak of Green,'" *EIR*, Jan. 29, 1999; Michele Steinberg, "The Conspirators in Gore's Cabinet," *EIR*, Feb. 5, 1999.

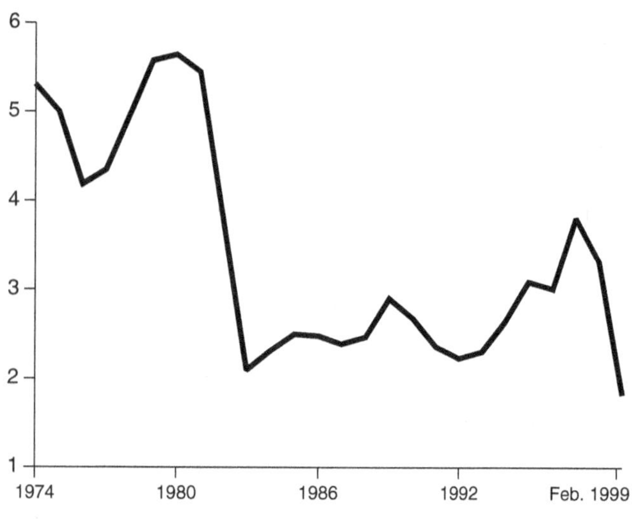

FIGURE 4
U.S. Machine Tool Production
(billions 1982 constant $)

Source: Association of Manufacturing Technology, *The Economic Handbook of the Machine Tool Industry*, various years; various sources; *EIR*.

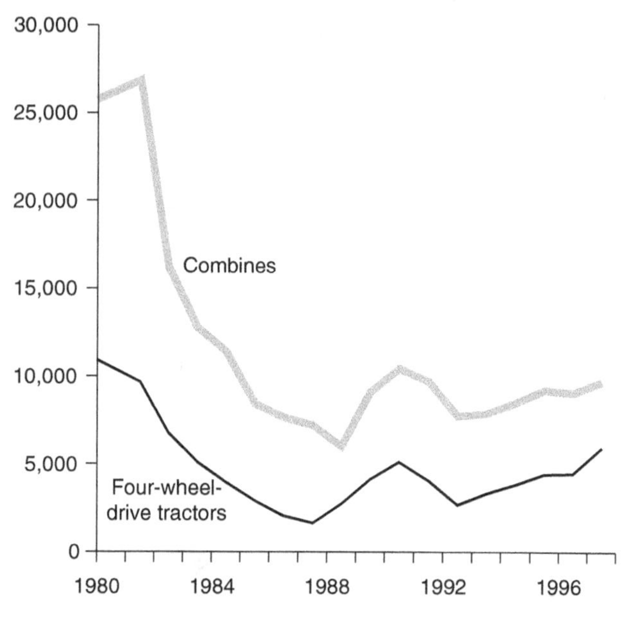

FIGURE 5
U.S. Shipments of Four-wheel-drive Tractors and Combines, 1980 to 1997
(number of units shipped)

Admittedly, the present, permanent national-debt crisis of the U.S. government, was created through Trilateral Commission policies rammed through under President Jimmy Carter. However, it was foolish Kemp-Roth, which caused Carter's national-debt bubble to zoom upward; this created the foundations of the present global "derivatives bubble." Kemp-Roth did this, by dumping the principles of the Franklin Roosevelt-modelled, Kennedy investment tax-credit, in favor of slashing the tax rates on purely parasitical forms of financial capital gains. Seeing how Kemp-Roth set this pattern, will help you to understand why the current rise of the Dow-Jones index depends upon destroying what remains today of the real economy of the U.S.A. and other nations.

The fact that the rate of mergers and acquisitions on a world scale, has skyrocketted at the rates seen during the first half of 1999, is one of those crucial facts, like Eddie George's gold scam, which warns sensible people that the world's financial system is at the verge of a melt-down—something with similarities to the model of a thermonuclear detonation.

The object of such junk-bond-style mergers and acquisitions, like the looting of the U.S. savings and loan industry by Trilateral Commission veteran and Vice-President George Bush's cronies, is to take over and loot banks and other industries, for the purpose of stripping away their salable assets, and leaving the emptied husk, as they did, on the doorsteps of those financial orphanages known as our bankruptcy and criminal courts.

They said the merger would make the economy better, by "trimming away fat"; actually, what the junk-bond raiders stole, was only what they considered "flesh and bone." Like Seventeenth- and Eighteenth-Century pirates seeking financial respectability in fashionable English countrysides, these modern emulators of the bloody old sea-raiders, used the "financial income-stream" generated by junk-bond-style and similar looting, to float highly leveraged financial capital gains on markets, thus transforming themselves from legally redeemed, sea-going night-riders, into persons, like the cronies of Britain's former Prime Minister Harold Wilson, claiming knightly honors as steadfast pillars of the financial community.

Looking at these effects of Garn-St Germain and Kemp-Roth together, shows quickly how those pieces of legislation dovetailed, to bring about the way in which that big swindle has worked, since 1982, up to the present time.

If we compare the combined effects of Carter Ad-

Industrial Energy Consumption per Household

(millions of BTUs)

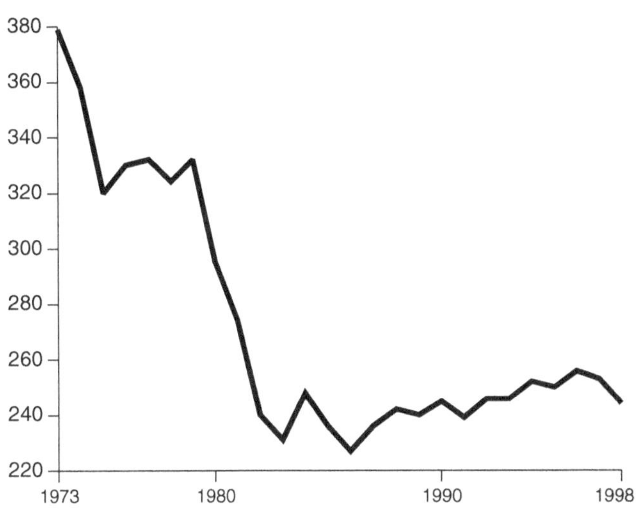

Sources: U.S. Department of Energy, *Monthly Energy Review*; U.S. Department of Commerce, Bureau of the Census, *Population Surveys, various years.*

U.S. Railroad Mileage

(miles per 1,000 households)

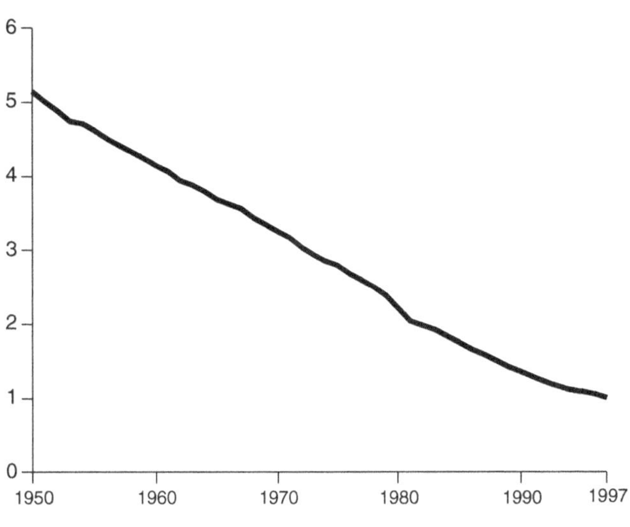

Sources: Association of American Railroads; U.S. Department of Commerce, Bureau of the Census, *Population Surveys*, various years.

ministration deregulation plus Garn-St Germain and Kemp-Roth, with what a post-1981 economy would have looked like under the Kennedy Administration's investment tax-credit and related pro-agro-industrial growth policies, we can quickly calculate a prosperous U.S. economy emerging from the Kennedy policies, as opposed to the catastrophic results produced by the combination of Nixon's post-August 15, 1971 "floating exchange-rate" folly and the combination of Carter Administration and Kemp-Roth-type follies of the 1980s.

If we take into account essential costs of maintaining preexisting levels of national productivity, which were taken off the books at various points since August 1971, and if we take into account the degree which the U.S. economy has limped along through its use of a "floating exchange-rate system" of traffic in international financial loans, to loot other nations, such as those of Central and South America, the U.S. national economy has not enjoyed a profit in net real output since about 1971.

Look at changes in the per-capita market-basket of purchasing power received per employee for a forty-hour work-week, compared with 1966-1970 levels. Look at savage cut-backs in maintenance of essential basic economic infrastructure, since 1971. Look at the catastrophic cut-backs in quality of education, in hospital-bed-days, and other essential services. Look at the increase in commuting time per week forced upon employees roaming ever further to increasing number of places of employment, per capita of labor-force. Look at the increased ratio of household debt to personal net income, per capita and per household. Look at the productive capacity and employees lost to "out-sourcing" and related looting of the earning-power, and physical productivity of the U.S. economy as a whole.

Look at the range of those domestic U.S. industrial facilities, which were indispensable in enabling the U.S.A. to put a man on the Moon in 1969, which have not existed any longer since years, even decades. [**Figures 8-10.**]

In part, the downward trend of a formerly successful U.S. economy, a downtrend institutionalized under Nixon and Carter, was to a significant degree a result of sheer stupidity about economics now widespread among the present generations' leading political and financier circles. It has also been, most emphatically, the result of sheer ideological lunacy, of the wild-eyed, utopian monetarism of the Mont Pelerin Society, lunacy of the Thatcherite variety.

That combined effect should call to our attention, the fact, that Mrs. Thatcher's record in economic matters, like that of Senator Phil Gramm, shows that the

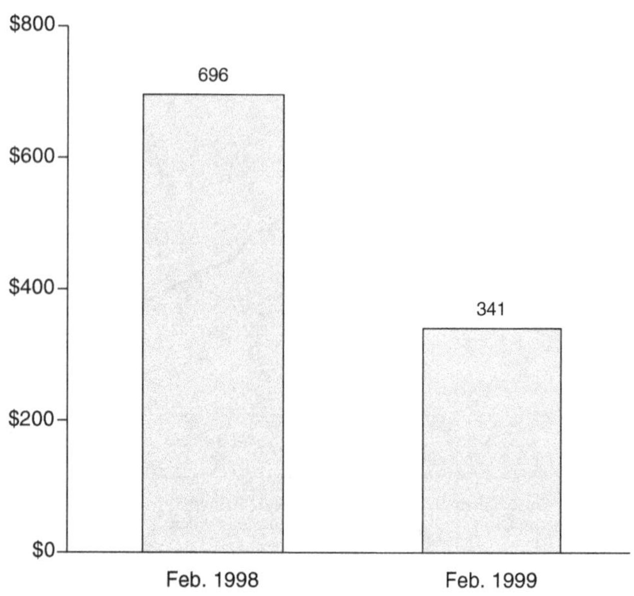

FIGURE 8

U.S. Machine Tool Consumption Collapses 51%, February 1998 vs. February 1999

(millions $)

Source: Association for Manufacturing Technology; American Machine Tool Distributors Association; *EIR*.

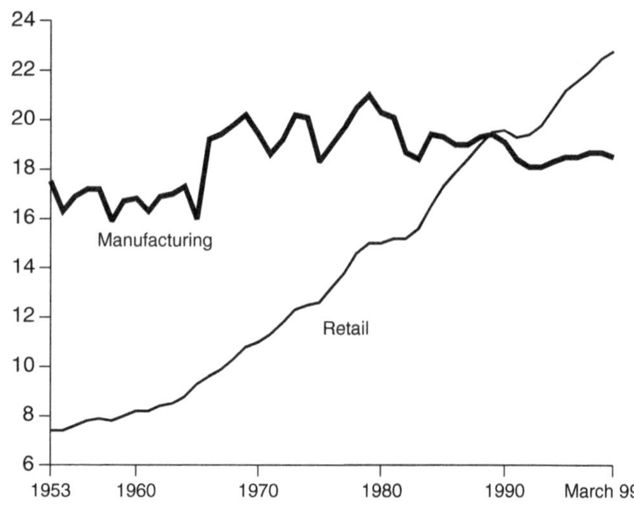

FIGURE 9

U.S. Retail Employment vs. Manufacturing Employment

(millions of jobs)

Sources: Bureau of Labor Statistics, U.S. Department of Labor, *Employment and Earnings,* various years; *Handbook of Labor Statistics.*

fact that certain politicians are nasty, does not necessarily mean that they are also intelligent. One should not be surprised that the results of putting such political figures into power, is usually a lot of nastiness, but, as Thatcher's long reign as Britain's Prime Minister also shows, very bad economic performance.

So, the Bush Leaguers, and other Trilateral Commission figures of the 1970s and 1980s, raped the U.S. economy, and set us up for the increasingly catastrophic state of world financial affairs since the Mexico crisis of 1994-1995.

2. The Solution

The key phrase, which brings justified hope to any nation suffering a general financial collapse, is the sound of those reassuring words: "After all, now that the system has collapsed, we can safely say that it was all really nothing more than just a lot of paper." Similarly, with the wondrous words, "You're all just a pack of cards!" Lewis Carroll's fictional Alice escaped to the safety of reality.

There is a lesson to be learned by Americans (and others) from the relative success of Russia's recent Primakov government, up to the point Primakov was ousted. The savage, IMF-directed looting of Russia during most of the past six years, had reduced that nation's economy to such a depleted state, that financial assets as such mean relatively very little today. As Primakov's government briefly demonstrated, by its notable few months of relative economic successes from doing nothing more than a few very sensible and obvious things, Russia has no choice, if it wishes to survive, but to forget about its ruined financial system, and the ruinous delusions of its so-called "liberals." Amid the ruins of the bankrupt, liberally destroyed present economic system, Russia is forced now to abandon the foolish advice of the bankrupt IMF system, and to rely instead, essentially, on the remaining, built-in physical-growth potentials of its physical economy.

The same will soon be clearly true for the United States, as it now proceeds, pathetically unprepared, to enter the next century.

Whether you are presently ready to believe it, or not, the fact is, that we in the United States are entering a situation not unlike that which struck Russia over 1992-1999 to date. Sooner than most of you will wish

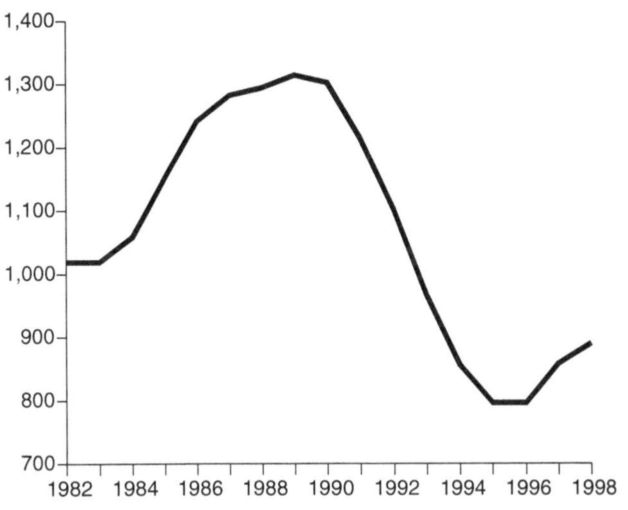

to believe, that fact will be brought home to you very soon. Then, you will curse the day that anyone ever suggested it would be better to have a "post-industrial society." Once you have finished your outbursts against the "post-industrial" freakishness, you will take a deep breath, and smile in relief. You will then smile, because you have realized that our situation need not be a hopeless one. "After all, it was just a lot of paper. Forget that paper, and now get on with our lives."

The solution is elementary in principle. Put all that foolish, failed paper into appropriate forms of government-supervised bankruptcy proceedings, set up a new credit, monetary, and financial system quickly, as Treasury Secretary Alexander Hamilton did so successfully. Get employment in real, physical output expanding quickly. Things will soon get better than they have been in decades. The key is: Don't cling to that sinking ship. It was only paper, and you were drowning in it, anyway.

The Measures To Be Taken

Therefore, certain facts must be stated to each of you, personally, as plainly as possible. As President Franklin Roosevelt understood he must say that, at a point of great, frightening national crisis, then, so I must say to you today: In the face of this global financial crisis, "we have nothing as much to fear, as fear itself." Therefore, someone must address you now so, again, as this terrible crisis is unfolding. For reasons which should not require much explanation, the respon-

sibility for saying the things needed to allay your fears, lies, for the moment, with me. It is I, for special reasons of the moment, who must explain certain things which I am best qualified professionally to say, both to you as citizens, and to the relevant officials of our government.

What I must say, will seem frightening at first. I must say it nonetheless, because it is the truth, and because you have the right and need to know the truth. Only when you see, that, terrible as the crisis is, there are happy solutions available, can you be kept free from the chaotic sorts of fears which might cause our nation's people and government alike, to be driven by fears into doing those sorts of desperate and foolish things which must be avoided.

Therefore, I must identify the problem. Admittedly, the truth is frightening. Nonetheless, you must hear that truth; my purpose is to show you the safe and calm way to walk out of something analogous to a burning theater. If we are to allay that greatest danger, "fear itself," we must face consciously the problem we are committed to solving.

For a benchmark, in planning the needed economic recovery, look back to an example from post-World War I Germany, up to the interval of Adolf Hitler's legal coups d'état of January 1933 and June-August 1934. Look at a Germany ruined by Versailles conditions similar to those recently imposed upon Russia by the IMF, that during 1992-1999 to date. Look at the 1923 Reichsmark hyperinflation, but concentrate now on two events from the interval 1931 through that London-directed, January 1933 coup d'état against the von Schleicher government, through which London, aided by the New York firm of Brown Brothers, Harriman, brought Hitler to power in Germany.

Look first, at a secret, 1931 Berlin, very high-level meeting of the pro-American System Friedrich List Society. At this meeting, at the prompting of economist Dr. Wilhelm Lautenbach, a recovery proposal was introduced and adopted, secretly, by the leading inner circles of Germany's patriots.[8] This recovery proposal began to be implemented under patriotic, anti-Hitler Chancellor Kurt von Schleicher. Had the Schleicher government, and its economic-recovery policies, not been overthrown, in favor of Adolf Hitler, by a British circle using von Papen, the recovery programs of the Schleicher government in Germany and of President-

---

8. Michael Liebig, "Lautenbach's Program for German Recovery," *EIR*, Jan. 8, 1999.

elect Franklin Roosevelt in the U.S.A., would have been largely identical in effect.[9] The Hitler regime, and the prolonged great Depression, the ensuing World War II, and the Nazi death-camps, would never have occurred.

Later, aspects of the same policies presented by Lautenbach in 1931, were adopted, with U.S. agreement, by German bankers under the leadership of Deutsche Bank's Hermann Abs. The result was the exceptionally successful "German economic miracle" of reconstruction, as associated with the now still-existing Kreditanstalt für Wiederaufbau.[10] The uniquely successful methods used, in these cases, was a consistent reflection of what is known world-wide as the American System of political-economy, the system associated by name with Alexander Hamilton, Mathew Carey, Friedrich List, and Henry C. Carey.

These are the methods, the proven precedent for success, which must be adopted again, to overcome what would be otherwise the worst, most prolonged economic depression in modern world history. Any sane person, who wishes to survive, will now absolutely rely upon insight into the fact, that nothing other than those proven, superior methods of economic recovery must be adopted and used afresh.

Remember: "It is only paper" that is falling now. That paper is the global economic cancer that is threatening the life of the United States, and also the world in general. Remove the cancer, to save the patient. Introduce the immune factors of economic policy needed to prevent that cancer of worthless speculative financial paper from growing back.

The first step, is to have a consortium, of several cooperating governments, each assert their perfect national sovereignty, and, declare, as their first joint action, the effectively global nullification of all forms of gambling debts such as "junk bonds" and "financial derivatives." That action, sweeping about $300 trillions-equivalent of purely parasitical, current debt from the world system, is the indispensable first step upon which escape from history's worst economic depression depends, absolutely, now. That debt, and related nominal financial assets, are to be swept away as if retroactively, as if they had never existed.

Clearing away that purely parasitical debt, in that way, is the absolute precondition for the survival of nations, including the U.S.A., today. A government which lacks the guts to do precisely that, in concert with a power-bloc composed of like-minded other governments, is in fact no government at all, and that would be made very clear, very soon, after the failure to seize the moment of opportunity to do what is absolutely necessary as a first step.

Following the declaration of the nullification of those categories of debt, the more or less simultaneous next step, is to organize a general, governments-directed bankruptcy-reorganization of other forms of indebtedness. In the case of the U.S.A. itself, the point of reference from which this is to be done, is nothing different than the 1789 U.S. Federal Constitution, especially the fundamental law of the U.S.A., as embodied in the Preamble of that Constitution, especially its so-called "general welfare clause." Other nations are well-advised to emulate this feature of the U.S. constitutional model.

On this account, there are two broad principles of practice to be served. First, the constitutional integrity of the U.S. Federal government itself must be defended by all of its patriots. Without that constitutional integrity of that perfectly sovereign authority, nothing else which is now essential would be feasible. Second, the methods used to conduct the financial reorganization of the hopelessly bankrupt U.S. financial sector, must be conducted in ways which best serve the constitutional mandate of the "general welfare clause."

That means, as U.S. Treasury Secretary Hamilton elaborated this policy, the integrity of the principal amount of the U.S. sovereign debt, principally the balance of the principal amount on the official debt of the U.S. Treasury, must be maintained.[11] Everything else is negotiable under government-supervised bankruptcy reorganization, that in ways which are in accord with the U.S. sovereign interest and primary internal constitutional obligations.

The latter consideration means, that every other aspect of financial reorganization must be subordinated to two objectives. First, the preconditions for an early and rapid general recovery of essential forms of physi-

9. Michael Liebig, "Recovery Program Could Have Blocked Hitler's 'Legal Coup,'" *EIR*, March 5, 1999. Speech to the Schiller Institute's Presidents' Day conference, Feb. 14, 1999.

10. Lothar Komp, "How Germany Financed Its Postwar Reconstruction," *EIR*, June 25, 1999.

11. Alexander Hamilton, *Report on Public Credit*, in **Papers on Public Credit, Commerce and Finance**, Samuel McKee, Jr., ed. (New York: Columbia University Press, New York, 1934).

cal production and distribution must be satisfied. Second, the general welfare of, especially, the weakest and most vulnerable portions of the population, must be defended as a matter of course. Consider the second requirement, first, before turning to other matters.

Insofar as personal savings, health-care provisions, and pensions are concerned, these claims must be met in full, up to some reasonably specified maximum amount for each individual case. Similar considerations apply to the working capital of socially essential institutions, including privately owned business institutions whose regular and orderly functioning is essential to the orderly maintenance of the well-being of the local populations. These and related provisions are given priority under what may be fairly described as "anti-chaos" measures. It must be the object of bankruptcy reorganization, that normal functioning of households and communities must be continued virtually from proverbial Day One of the placing of the national economy under the protection of generalized bankruptcy-reorganization.

Otherwise, the general rule for initial phases of generalized financial-bankruptcy reorganization, is to freeze everything else in sight, and to organize a controlled release of funds, either as loans or otherwise, against the principal value of sums relegated to frozen accounts. The general rule, is that useful production and distribution of needed physical goods, must be uninterrupted, and that essential institutions remain standing and functional, even if they might be judged as insolubly bankrupt. Keep things which must function, functioning, and sort out the financial accounts at leisure.

Take the case of bankrupt local banks, for an example.

A local bank is a place of deposit for local citizens and local firms, and an instrument through which loans and other essential financial services to the community are administered. Thus, even in the case the local bank were totally insolvent, its function and related operations must (usually) be continued as if it were a fully sovereign institution. The preferred object of bankruptcy reorganization of such banks, is to keep the bank alive and functioning as a working institution of the local community, and, hopefully, to restore it to financial independence through some process of financial reorganization.

In other words, the policy must be, to keep all essential features of national functioning and community life working, as if without missing a step, in the transition from a state of seemingly hopeless national financial bankruptcy, into a fully functioning society with a fully functioning economy, but an economy stripped down, for the moment, to bare essentials of continued defense of national security and of the general welfare.

Organizing Economic Growth

The United States, as a national economy, is, like most of the other nations of the world, presently financially bankrupt. It is bankrupt, in part, because of a parasitical form of financial bubble; but, it is also bankrupt, because, in net effect, it is not currently producing enough to meet even its own internal needs. So far, we have focussed on the first cause of that condition of bankruptcy. Now, we must address the second.

Focus upon the third, the lower, of the three curves of my Triple Curve representation, as shown above, of a typical collapse function. As measured in real, physical-economic, rather than the merely nominal, financial, yardsticks of our super-polluted present financial system, the U.S. economy has been declining over the course of the recent thirty years. This decline began, during 1966-1971, as a relative decline in the net rate of real economic growth. After 1971, and, especially since 1976, there has been a persisting net absolute collapse of the economy over the entire period 1977-1999 to date. This point is made clear, when we examine the sundry ways, by means of which the U.S.A. has used the present, post-1971 form of the IMF system, the so-called "floating-exchange-rate" system, and globalized financial deregulation, as a way of looting other nations to bail out a self-inflicted U.S. national economy itself.

The use of a fraudulent system of IMF-coordinated "international financial loans," to loot the nations of Central and South America, repeatedly, over the 1971-1999 interval, is typical of the looting operation involved. The use of "out-sourcing," as a way of looting nations such as Mexico, to subsidize the U.S. economy, while also destroying the economy and productive employment of the population living inside the U.S.A., is another relevant example. Such is the looting-process run, essentially, in cooperation between the world's dominant financial system, the London-centered British Commonwealth system, London's junior financial partner, Wall Street, and what U.S. hero General Smedley Butler exposed as Wall Street's usurpation of control over the U.S. military establishment.

In short, even if we eliminate the crushing debt-burden caused by the cumulative follies of U.S. policy over the recent thirty years, we have not eliminated the fact that we are currently producing at levels, which have been driven down, during the recent thirty-odd years, to a point way below that needed to maintain the kind of average standard of living and per-capita productivity, which we had achieved during the middle to late 1960s. Getting rid of the financial parasite, is indispensable, but not sufficient. Additional measures of economic recovery are needed, even merely to bring the nation back up to break-even levels of physical-economic input and output.

Let us look at this problem in the simpler way any reasonably literate and intelligent U.S. citizen might understand what we are talking about here.

Go back to the early years of the U.S. post-war economy, 1946-1955. Then, compare relevant figures from that period with the Kennedy economic recovery, 1961-1963, from the Eisenhower period's slide, under Arthur Burns' influence, into a deep, stubbornly prolonged recession, 1956-1960.[12] Look at the periods 1946-1955, and 1961-1963, as setting a bench-mark of comparison for studying the relevant downturn in the U.S. economy since 1967-1972. Use this bench-mark as a way of gaining rule-of-thumb qualities of insight into the qualitative degeneration of the structure of employment of the U.S. labor-force since 1967-1972, most emphatically during and following the ruinous effects of the interval 1977-1982.

For this purpose, we are obliged to place the emphasis on categories of composition of the raw employment of the total labor-force. After 1972, Gross National Product and National Income statistics, are polluted, increasingly, by effects of the pyramiding of fictitious capitalization, and, therefore, of the costs attributed (i.e., as incurred by) to that capitalization. After 1982, the official U.S. government and Federal Reserve statistical reports are so transparently, but chaotically faked for purposes of "political spin," that such official sources no longer represent an even approximately ac-

---

12. The deep Eisenhower recession, is defined, more narrowly, as from February 1957 through mid-1958. However, the recession of 1957 was triggered by a lunatic consumer-credit bubble of 1956, and the effects of the recession were continued beyond the Summer of 1958, into election-year 1960.

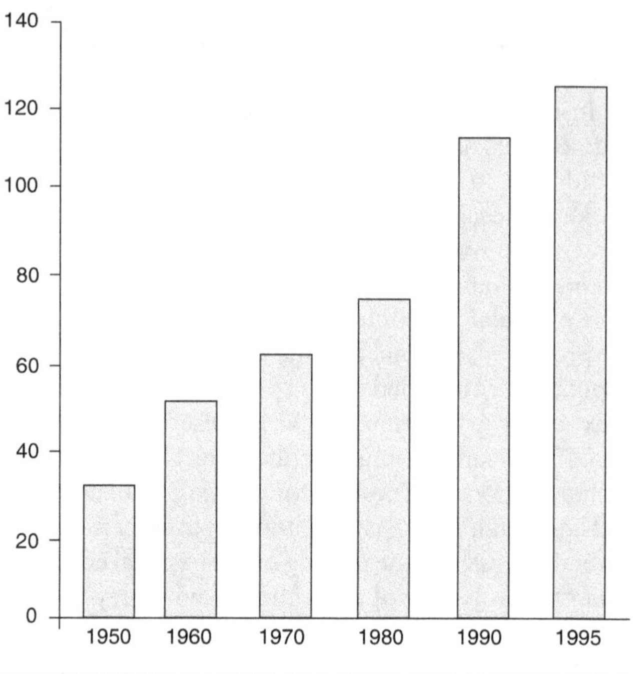

curate time-series. An insightful study of structural composition of employment of the total labor-force, is therefore the best first-approximation indicator of the relevant changes to be considered here.

Two aspects of overall patterns of employment must be kept in mind. First, there is the matter of employment in direct generation of output; second, there is employment related to the maintenance and increase of the physical-economic form of capital-intensity of production and its output. In the capital goods sector, the machine-tool sector is of crucial importance, and the smaller-sized machine-tool-design sector, and equivalent kinds of capital-goods-related functions, the most crucial.

Those noted qualifications listed, compare the composition of employment according to the broad following categories. Development and maintenance of basic economic infrastructure (hard), basic economic infrastructure (soft)—such as health-care and education, transport of physical goods, agriculture, manufacturing, services performed by the physical-science and engineering professions, employment categories which were traditional prior to 1967, and those which have blossomed as side-effects of "post-industrial" fads of

U.S. Labor Force, 1970-99; Non-productive Overhead Grows

(millions of workers)

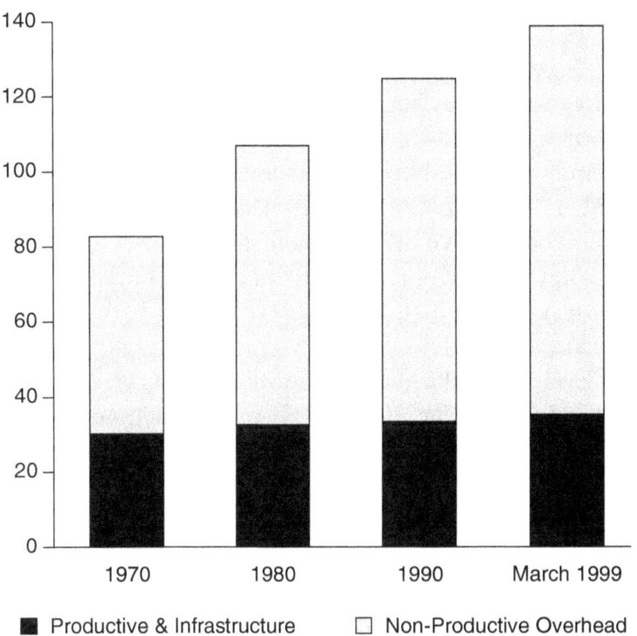

Sources: Bureau of Labor Statistics, Department of Labor; U.S. Department of Education; American Medical Association.

the recent thirty years. [**Figures 11-12**.]

The changes shown by such comparison of structural changes in composition of employment, point to the reasons why, first, the U.S. economy is presently operating way below physical-economic breakeven levels, by comparison with 1966-1971, and, second, what kinds of changes must be made to reverse that decline.

This, in itself, is an area of major topics of policy deliberations. Therefore, what I shall offer here are merely some crucial illustrations of the policy-issues which a genuine physical-economic recovery involves.

A genuine economic-recovery policy requires that government adopts certain general policy objectives governing its role in fostering a relatively rapid, feasible rate of net physical-economic growth, above what might be described as a "break-even" level of structural composition of labor-force employment. In general, we must emphasize a leading role of expanded development of presently much-depleted basic economic infrastructure in fostering a "New Deal" style of employ-

ment-driven physical-economic recovery, an increasing ratio of capital formation in agriculture and manufacturing, and increasing levels of employment in manufacturing, especially in high-technology enriched capital-goods products. This also means an emphasis on greatly increased power generation, and emphasis upon capital-intensive and power-intensive modes of advancement of technology in product design and modes of production.

It means, on the other side, a slashing of employment in parasitical categories such as so-called financial services and other post-1967 changes in the nature and relative quantity of employment in unskilled, or low-skilled services.

Government has two general means, in addition to consultation, to foster such changes in structural composition of employment. One is public policy respecting flows of credit; the second, is taxation policy. The Kennedy investment tax-credit policy supplies a useful standard of comparison for defining a useful sort of tax policy: a tax policy premised upon an appropriate notion of the preferences dictated by clear national interest.

To conduct such a recovery program under the conditions we must foresee for the beginning of the coming century, there must be a clear understanding of the difference between issuing money, and issuing credit. Through the proper application of public credit for fostering programs of economic growth in the national interest, the progress payments made in connection with those programs generates an increase in the income and tax-revenue bases of the national economy. This expansion of the income and tax-revenue base expands the platform for launching an enlarged flow of credit. On the condition, that the programs selected for such assigned priorities, have the effect of increasing national income, both per capita and per square kilometer, a self-feeding spiral of real economic growth can be sustained indefinitely.

As part of this, the responsibility of a recovery policy by government must be, not to foster the recovery of levels of employment in relatively undesirable categories of the present structure, while fostering increases in employment in the relatively most desirable categories, those which contribute relatively the most to the scale and rate of productivity of output of the nation's physical economy, per capita and per square kilometer.

We have done that before, several times in our nation's history. We can, and must do it again.

3. Zero-Sum Brains

Now, you must look inside yourself, to discover there, inside yourself, those bad habits of thought which might cause you yourself to contribute to ruining our nation's chance of survival.

Did you know, that Alan Greenspan, the Chairman of the Federal Reserve System, has bragged publicly that he is clinically insane?[13] Did you know, that many among the world's leading bankers and other financial houses, are also victims of the same form of clinical insanity which Alan Greenspan has claimed to be suffering?[14] Did you know that many of the highest-paid stratum of people in Wall Street, are suffering the same form of mass insanity exhibited by those caught with their derivatives down, when LTCM crashed, last September? This is not a case of a new variety of "sexually transmitted diseases." Although apparently infectious, the disease is purely psychological. The form of mass insanity suffered by each and all of these fools, is best identified as "the zero-sum brain" syndrome.

All of those persons to whom I have just pointed, as clinically insane, were trapped by their own delusions, as "true believers" in a world which does not exist. All were caught, financial red-ink-handed, in a lunatic cult, known as the Black-Scholes formula, the Nobel Prize-winning insanity for which Robert C. Merton and Myron S. Scholes were awarded the 1997 Nobel Prize in economics.[15] This was the formula which engineered the collapse of the Long Term Capital Management hedge-fund.

"So what?" a representative of the Nobel Prize committee said, in effect, when this result of the Merton-Scholes award was pointed out to him by *EIR*. He claimed, that the Nobel Prize committee had never intended, that admirers of Merton's and Scholes' formulations could have been so dumb, as to overlook the fact that the Prize-winners' mathematics is only an academic game, which does not correspond to the real world.

Even after the experience of the LTCM collapse, last year, this year, June 10-11, to be exact, and, more recently, this July, have rolled around. Leading hedge-funds and their bankers have been freshly exposed by these recent developments, as having played the same financially suicidal game, bigger and worse than ever, which they had played, with such nearly fatal results, in the Spring through Summer of 1998.

In other words, all those victims of the zero-sum-brain syndrome, fell prey to their own personal clinical insanity. At last report, most among both the world's biggest banks, and the central bankers of most nations, are even more insane today, than they were in August and September of 1998. There are no signs that their mental health is about to improve.

Unfortunately, most investors in mutual funds, when the funds go down, will also have to be diagnosed as victims of the same form of mass insanity.

So far, this form of insanity is controlling not only those bankers and financial houses. Up to this moment of writing, the governments of the G-7 nations, like the International Monetary Fund and World Bank, are being controlled, politically, by this same, currently fashionable, Wall Street style in lunacy.

The biggest chunk of contributors to the Year 2000 Presidential pre-candidacies of both George W. Bush and his patsy, Vice-President Al Gore, come from the same big Wall Street set of "irrationally exuberant," "zero-sum gang-bangers" involved in the LTCM and similar—past, present, and future—hedge-fund catastrophes. These are also among the biggest contributors

---

13. E.g., Alan Greenspan, testimony before the House Subcommittee on Finance and Hazardous Materials, Committee on Commerce, March 3, 1999, titled "On Investing the Social Security Trust Fund in Equities": "The transfer of Social Security assets from U.S. Treasuries to equities would not, in itself, have any effect on national saving. Thus, the underlying economic assets in the economy would be unchanged, as would the total income generated by those assets. Any increase in returns realized by Social Security must be offset by a reduction in returns earned on private portfolios, which represent, to a large extent, funds held for retirement. Investing Social Security assets in equities is, then, largely a zero-sum game. To a first approximation, aggregate retirement resources—from both Social Security and private funds—do not change."

14. I refer to a list of leading world banks and their associates in the operations of the Long Term Capital Management (LTCM) hedge-fund, which was bailed out—at your expense—with the help of Alan "your money" Greenspan's Federal Reserve System, during September 1998. Banks known to have been caught in the LTCM crash include: Bankers Trust, Bank of Italy, Barclays, Bear Stearns, Chase Manhattan, Citigroup, Crédit Agricole, Crédit Suisse First Boston, Deutsche Bank, Goldman Sachs, ING Barings, J.P. Morgan, Lehman Brothers, Merrill Lynch, Morgan Stanley Dean Witter, Paribas, Société Générale, and UBS. (This list includes all banks that participated in the bail-out, and a few who didn't, but had money in LTCM.)

15. John Hoefle, "One Derivatives Disaster After Another: Will They Never Learn?," *EIR*, Oct. 9, 1998.

to right-wing conservative congressional campaigns, and so on and so forth.

The facts are, that the situation is much worse than those facts, by themselves, would indicate. Much of the pro-deregulation legislation being pushed through the Congress now, has been, in effect, bought and paid for by the same pack of Wall Street loonies caught in the LTCM crash. Being the kind of Democrat who is bought and paid for by the same Wall Street desperadoes' influence, is what Vice-President Al Gore has called "The Third Way."

Everything the U.S. and other G-7 governments did, from the Washington, D.C. September conference, on, has shown itself to be a case of colossal folly by each and all of the governments and monetary institutions complicit in those agreements. They each and all agreed to continue to run the world economy according to the rules of the game invented by the world's biggest lunatics, the zero-sum game. As a result, the crisis is far more hopeless today, than it was in October 1998; the real economy has shrunk at the fastest rate in the past thirty years; only the financial bubble and the fools have become bigger.

So, when the present world financial system goes down in a bust, as it will soon, it will be that form of mass clinical insanity which will have been chiefly responsible for the crash.

How Do You Define Insanity?

Pause, for just a moment, at this point. Some readers will object: "Okay, so, I admit: those guys were living in a fantasy-world. Lots of people spend a lot of time occupied by their variously childish or adolescent styles in fantasy-life; that doesn't mean that all of them are necessarily insane."

True! Then, what is the difference between a bit of dabbling in fantasy, even a lot of it, over the course of the day, and being actually insane? The difference between day-dreaming and insanity, is that the day-dreamer still benefits from being capable of distinguishing between fantasy and reality, even if he has to be pushed, sometimes, into reluctant admission of that fact. When the dreamer resists all reasonable efforts to bring him back to reality, his influence within society should be considered as that of a functionally insane person, such as Alan Greenspan.

Admittedly, there are border-line cases, cases which have not yet crossed that border line, into outright insanity. Consider some commonplace, functional types of border-line cases.

Take the case of high-powered super-salesmen, for example, whose ability to lull buyers into admiring the salesman's show of "deep conviction," is responsible for the sad ending likely to be suffered by the mutual funds or other sort of customer.[16] That sort of salesman, while he is selling, blocks reality out of his, or her mind. He, or she, constructs what is adopted as a persuasive fantasy. The target of this attempted seduction is intended to perceive, that the sales representative is so much "in love" with the prospect, that the customer is persuaded that such a loving and important person would never do his customer wrong.

Such sales types (the legendary type who might sell ice-cubes to the Eskimos in winter-time) will often express their view, if only privately, that "I could not sell" unless the selling were motivated by such a fantasy-life. ("Don't pop my fantasy-bubble, or I won't be able to sell in the morning, and, then, we'll all go hungry!" such a poor fellow may scream at his wife.) Away from the selling territory, they come back to some sense of everyday real life, if only in small matters, but such returns to reality do not occur without the hangover-like emotional effect of sobering up after a fantasy-binge.

Similar patterns are to be observed in the cases among even learned professions whose professional activities, performed as personal services, involve resort to the salesman-like musterings of the "bedside manner," as this is practiced by those among today's professional, truth-hating perverts known as "facilitators." We shall turn attention to a very special importance of this problem of a "services"-oriented economy, a bit later here.

The salesman-type I have described, is highly neurotic, but that does not, by itself, signify that he or she is actually insane. The cross-over to clinical insanity, occurs at the point the fantasy-ridden individual, such as Alan Greenspan, Professor Milton Friedman, Zbigniew Brzezinski, or Jeffrey Sachs, makes the cross-over, away from recognition of the existence of a real

---

16. Decades ago, during the 1950s and 1960s, I did a series of precautionary studies of this sort of salesman behavior, in an effort to weed out this common cause of avoidable customer complaints against the firms employing the relevant sales personnel. Companies which were too easily impressed by the front-end side of the sales performance of such representatives, often let themselves be blinded into the medium- to long-term costs of the after-effects of the same salesman performance they had admired at the time the sale was initially closed.

world, to dwell entirely within a mind-set which is inherently of the form of a destructive fantasy-life. The operative term is "destructive."[17]

Alan Greenspan's Zero-Sum Mind

In this case, as typified by Alan Greenspan, we are focussed on a special form of a process of crossing-over from the sickly state of a mind which is richly polluted by its fantasy-life, to outright insanity. We are focussed on the specific clinical form of insanity identified as the case of "the zero-sum mind."

As the case of Eddie George's gold scam makes the point, under conditions of severe stress, such as a general financial crisis, this pathological syndrome tends toward outrightly criminal insanity. The form of such insanity—and criminality—on which we are focussed, is the gambler's mind-set, as typified by the lunatic belief that a national, or world economy, is something so characteristically inhuman—better said, so anti-human, so essentially fascist—as a variety of what von Neumann defined as a zero-sum game. That is the focus of my subject here.

As in much of the ordinary neurotic's childish or adolescent forms of fantasy-life, the fantasy-ridden person is a *symbol*-minded creature, like the putative inventor of the zero-sum game—who happens to have been, not that mastermind who recently claimed to have invented the "Internet," Al Gore, but the late John von Neumann. Like most childish fantasies, the symbol-minded idea of the zero-sum game, may become, like its cousin, the assembled masses at an Adolf Hitler Nuremberg rally, highly complicated in detail of its organization, but is a product of a state of mind, like that of Wall Street's master-minded Al Gore, which is in no way capable of profound and truthful, actually human thought. All symbol-minded fantasies of this childish or adolescent type, have the characteristics of games which children and sports-fanatics "make up." Sometimes, such fantasies become complicated, but they are always superficial, nonetheless, never part of the real world.

The linear mathematics of LTCM's Black-Scholes formula, is such a game. It represents a form of constructing a chain-letter form of bubble, a fantasy-life. That linear fantasy-life serves the deranged mind as a substitute for the real world. This is one of the factors which, all too often, causes so-called "pure mathematicians" to turn obviously insane and withdrawn, even at a young age when they should be outgoing, witty, and pleasantly frisky. In the case of John von Neumann's behavior, when he was confronted personally with the disproof of his life's work by Kurt Gödel, the lifelong burden of his enraged reaction, from that point on, through the remaining decades of his tormented life, typifies the psychosis-tending personality disorders not rare among such cases.[18]

The same pathology is reflected among young computer programmers and related specialists, or among avid addicts of a game of the form of Go. Video games are high-risk behavior, on this specific account. In those games, the pre-programmed engagement of childish passions is led toward the point, that the addicted personality becomes emotionally disassociated from the real world. One might compare such behavioral situations to those risks of desensitization to be overcome by a mind living within the life-support system of a time-capsule, or, exposed to the "cabin fever" of long-term interplanetary flight.

Indeed, typical psychosis is a model of the state of mind which such pathological environments—such as "sensory deprivation"—tend to induce among what would have been, otherwise, more or less healthy personalities. Look at the case of Wall Street's symbol-minded economists from this vantage-point.

The axiomatic distinction of various such problems

---

17. The significance of the qualifying term, "destructive," is that if a bad habit shows no destructive effects, the victim of an illusion lacks the kind of evidence which would force him to recognize the factual moral or other sort of wrongness of his ostensibly harmless form of errant habitual opinion. It is when an habitual opinion persists in opposition to clear evidence of destructive, or self-destructive results, that the red line separating ordinary delusions from functional sanity is defined in practical terms.

18. Von Neumann sat in the room where mathematician Gödel presented a conclusive proof, exposing as a fraud Bertrand Russell's principal theorem of linear mathematics. This was the merely conjectured theorem, which Russell disciple von Neumann had adopted as his life's work. "Johnny" von Neumann took Gödel's good news with a sweet smile, but, later, privately, admitted, and exhibited his bitter hatred against Gödel's success. "Johnny" reacted to this set-back, by leaving serious mathematics, for the favorite mathematical sport of Paolo Sarpi's household lackey Galileo, the linear mathematical theory of gambling games. "Johnny" spent the remainder of his life chiefly in dedication to proving that every economy, even the workings of the human mind itself, could be reduced to terms of curve-fitting models based upon methods for solutions for systems of simultaneous linear inequalities. From this came such derivatives as the fatal folly of the Black-Scholes formula. Another Russell disciple, and Hilbert reject, Norbert Wiener, showed similar fits of obsessive rage when crossed on similar points of Russell-like doctrine.

of this same general class, whether as the root of psychosis, or merely pathological forms of fantasy-life, is the substitution of mere symbols for physical reality. This sort of pathological syndrome appears commonly on one, or both of two levels. It occurs in a relatively more subtle form, in the tendency of the cognitively illiterate, to substitute blind faith in the reality of those mere symbols known as sense-impressions, for physical reality. It appears in the more radical, more vicious form, as in the case of the person whose study of formal mathematics leads him into a state of virtual psychosis, where the use of mere symbols is carried to the extremes of the modern logical positivist, such as von Neumann, or Merton and Scholes, with whom empty symbols are substituted for even sense-impressions.

In economics, the common expression of such Lockean empiricist's or logical positivists' tendencies for psychotic forms of behavior, is the substitution of money for physical-economic reality. Typical of the pathological extreme to which this pathological state of mind is carried among the population in general, is the legendary, rather commonplace case of what is so obviously a mentally unbalanced housewife, as she who retorts, "I don't have to worry about what happens to the farmers. I get my milk from the supermarket"—or, "my bread from the Internet." She has substituted mere symbols, the notion of cash, or perhaps only a credit-card, at the counter, the "magic of the marketplace," for the human production of reality. She is exhibiting a more extreme form of the insanity, which impelled formerly wealthy stock-traders to jump from Wall Street buildings back in 1929. For what did they jump—for Hecuba, perhaps? For symbols on paper! For the sake of pieces of paper which had suddenly revealed to their symbol-minded possessor, that they were still, after all, nothing but paper. That is the form of clear-cut insanity on which I am focussing your attention here.

In economics, von Neumann's notion of a zero-sum game, begins with the purely arbitrary, and false assumption, that economy, whether in the mode of barter, or monetary exchange, starts with some fixed magnitude. Thereafter, one person's gain is presumed to occur only as someone else's loss. What is outlawed by von Neumann's deranged mind, is the notion that the buyer may gain from the productive use of that which is supplied by another, that the economy is caused to grow by the productive use of that which may be purchased. That, thus, in such exchanges between A and B, neither A nor B loses, but both may enjoy a gain which might appear in their accounts as profit, without diminishing anything which is the other's.

Thus, the characteristic mental derangement of an Alan Greenspan, is the assumption that derivatives can not be bad, because what one speculator might lose, is offset more or less exactly by what some other speculator has gained.

Your Escape to Sanity

What is the alternative to such forms of symbol-mindedness? Where is the reality lurking behind the illusions which each generalized financial collapse, such as 1929's, exposes as having been "nothing but paper falling"? The point to be made is, in essentials, one I have presented, repeatedly, in earlier locations. Therefore, it is sufficient to summarize the core of the argument here.

Money is nothing more than *a medium of exchange*. It has no inherent propensity to grow of its own accord. The fact that a charge may be made for the loan of mere money, does not mean that mere money actually earns a profit in the sense of causing, of generating such profit in the real world existing outside the domain of mere paper.

The common academic use of the word "utility," as that usage was introduced by certain British and Viennese economists, is essentially a hoax, a fraud. The fact that money has a usefulness as a medium of exchange, does not imply that money itself commands any gain other than compensation for the actual costs of printing and circulating the stuff in ways which a medium of exchange may, as merely a medium of exchange, facilitate employment, production, and trade. Money has no sane claim to any pre-assigned or other "natural" rate of profit, rent, or interest. Money itself could not produce anything which would generate such a margin of gain in the real—that is, physical—economy.

Money is never more than a political fiction. In any sane national economy, money is circulated as a legal medium of exchange solely by the sovereign authority of some sovereign nation-state.

In the history of the U.S.A., the first such issuance of money was by the Seventeenth-Century Massachusetts Bay Colony. The manner of creation and use of that currency is explained by Cotton Mather,[19] and also,

---

19. Cotton Mather, *Some Considerations on Bills of Credit* (Boston, 1691). See H. Graham Lowry, *How The Nation Was Won: America's Untold Story* (Washington, D.C.: Executive Intelligence Review, 1988),

later, by Benjamin Franklin.[20] It was issued solely to serve as a medium of exchange, issued to promote trade, and therefore increase volumes of production of useful goods.[21]

Such sovereign issue of currency is created for circulation by that sovereign government, which pledges its political power and authority to give negotiable value to that currency. It is the power, and willful commitment of that state to defend the value of its currency, that by means including sundry protectionist measures, which establishes and maintains the currency's value in terms of physical goods. The purpose of the issuance of such currency, is not to promote trade; it is, as in the case of the Massachusetts Bay Colony, to promote an increase of production by facilitating trade. It is this production, not the mere trade in produced articles, which underlies the value represented by money in trade.

The proper form for issuance of money is, in the first instance, as credit extended by the sovereign government. This credit is issued to promote useful employment, development of basic economic infrastructure, increase of the scale of agricultural and industrial employment, and so on. The issue of state-created credit for purchases on government account, or as loans, must then be supported by the issue of currency at the place where the credit issued in the form of a government contract (such as a check) is presented for cash payment.

The usefulness of money placed in circulation, as a medium of exchange, will usually ensure that the added amount of such money put into circulation will be but a fraction of the total production and circulation of goods effected through the original emission of government credit. That customary relationship breaks down only when some crisis of the financial system, such as that under way today, intervenes to produce a contrary effect.

The intrinsic worth represented by that currency will never be anything other than a reflection of the volume and rate of increase of productive employment and output of produced goods in that national economy, per capita and per square kilometer.

Take the case of current disputes over the funding of reconstruction of the war-ravaged Balkans. What is said on this subject by sundry G-7 governments and relevant international institutions, is insane babble, when compared with the actual requirements for such a reconstruction program. The idiotic babble assumes the form of the expressed, ignorant assumption, that the launching of a reconstruction program estimated at a certain amount in results, requires the issue of a corresponding amount of money advanced as contributions.

In reality, any sane reconstruction program is financed not by loan of money, but by issuance of created state credit, credit created by the various assisting and assisted governments involved. The credit is issued as letters of state credit, not money, to those parties which contract to fulfill the relevant elements of the reconstruction program. These issued credits will be supported, eventually, by minimal interest-rate loans, of maturities of up to between twenty and thirty years maturity. Much of the state credit issued to launch the reconstruction program, will be offset by the long-term loans charged to recipient economies, or to the privately owned enterprises and other assets which are created as benefits of the reconstruction effort.

The role of Germany's Kreditanstalt für Wiederaufbau, in steering the exemplary success of post-war reconstruction, is a model of the way in which repeated rollover of a relatively small amount of initial issue of state credit, can produce a very large amount of resulting reconstruction.

So much for the matter of currency and credit itself. We are now free to address the heart of the matter.

The fundamental principles underlying the function of all economies, are peculiarities of human individual and social behavior inhering in those qualities which

p.40.

20. Benjamin Franklin, *A Modest Inquiry Into the Nature and Necessity of Paper Currency* (1729), reprinted in Nancy Spannaus and Christopher White, eds., ***The Political Economy of the American Revolution***, second edition (Washington, D.C.: Executive Intelligence Review, 1996).

21. These arguments by Mather and Franklin represent the precedents for the use of money under the U.S. Federal Constitution. This was in contrast to the money-systems of Europe. It must be taken into account, that, by definition, no parliamentary form of government constitutes a sovereign republic. Parliamentary government of the European model, even to the present day, is a relic of feudalism, not a product of the establishment of sovereign nation-state republics corresponding to the model of the U.S. 1789 Federal Constitution. The parliaments developed as popular encroachments upon the authority of the preexisting form of state power. The relationship between the state power of the United Kingdom, exclusive to the monarchy itself, and the elected parliament, overturned at the pleasure of the monarchy, is typical of European parliamentary systems generally. Thus, the traditional currency and central banking systems of European parliamentary governments have a different legal basis than are consistent with our original Federal Constitution.

set the human species absolutely apart from, and above all other living species. This distinction, is that non-deductive quality of cognition through which, among other results, mankind is able to generate validated discoveries of universal physical principles. It is these discoveries of validatable universal principles, which enable the human species, uniquely, to increase its power within and over the universe. This increase is reflected, inclusively, in increases of man's increases in his own demographically expressed physical power to exist, as reflected in demographic characteristics of both family households and populations in general, and in the increase of man's power over nature, per square kilometer of the Earth's surface. These increases are expressed in terms of what I have defined as *potential relative population-density.*

Thus, the essence of economy is expressed primarily in terms of the increase of man's physical power over nature. The rate of gain of that power, as measurable primarily in per-capita and per-square-kilometer terms, is the source of true profit. It is the rate of that gain, relative to the previously established scale, which represents a definable physical-economic value, independent of the notion of a money-value.

Thus, the value of milk is expressed both as the importance of milk to the changing physical-economic characteristics of the population as a whole, and as the cost of producing and maintaining the farming operations which produce that milk. Or, the value of public education, is the rate of increase of the productivity of the population as a whole, as measured in physical-economic, rather than monetary terms.

For example, the most significant portion of the total physical-economic activity of a modern economy, is the development and maintenance of the basic economic infrastructure of the surface-area taken as a unified whole. By the nature of that task, competent such development and maintenance could not occur, except as a direct economic activity of the government, rather than private entrepreneurship, or by government-regulated public utilities. This state role in the economy, is thus the largest and most highly capitalized section of healthy modern national economies.

The so-called private sector, is more or less indispensable, because the generation of technologies depends upon the leading role of those specific types of entrepreneurs who translate scientific and technological progress into those designs and modes of production which are the cutting edge of realized rates of growth of productivity. Yet, without basic economic infrastructure's functional development of the land-area in which entrepreneurial gains in productivity are to be realized, productivity gains will be stifled, just as good seeds may be ruined for lack of pre-developed crop-growing fields.

It is the physical relationship of the population as a whole, to its own perpetuation through the development of the productive land-area as a whole, which is the domain of real economy. The driver of that domain, is the development and employment of the cultivated cognitive powers of the individual person. It is in this way, that the modern sovereign nation-state excels far above any other conceivable form of social organization, in promoting the maintenance and improvement of mankind's power in, and over the universe.

The rest is only paper.

Between the Cracks

Why must empiricists such as John Locke, or positivists such as John von Neumann be considered as necessarily functionally insane? It is not that such empiricists and positivists might prove to be insane sometimes. In certain crucial respects, any empiricist or positivist is intrinsically insane, when such beliefs and practices are judged in functional terms. The reason for this curious coincidence lies, so to speak, between the cracks of both sense-impressions and symbols.

The issue is the same I have addressed in earlier locations, the form of delusions consistent with the absurd belief that that universe itself is organized according to the false, but popular axiomatic belief, that the physical universe can be accurately represented mathematically according to the assumption that causality is organized in a way which is congruent with the notion that everything is linear in the infinitesimally small.

Thus, when the empiricist screams, "But, I have the facts!" he is engaged in perpetrating the deception that the phenomena which he chooses to refer as "facts," are linked together physically by a principle of simple linearity in the infinitesimally small. In other words, his fraud lies in the screaming fact, that he is playing the childish game of "connect the dots." The dots to which he refers, may be real phenomena, but his fraud lies in the fact that he is insisting that you buy his wild presumption that those dots are necessarily connected by straight lines.

In economic science, the important facts are not objects, but those *changes* in the picture of the economy brought about through those kinds of changes in human behavior which are not limited to, but typified by scientific and technological progress. This idea of change is typified by the statement, in economic science, that the primary empirical fact is the study of increases, or decreases of the physical-economic productive powers of labor, per capita, and per square kilometer. It is the *connection* among those changes themselves, not a connection among the dots of sense-perception, which is the primary subject-matter of economics as Gottfried Leibniz defined it, as a branch of physical science.

Therefore, you must ask, "What is that connection?" The connection is the unique power of the cultivated individual human mind, to generate an experimentally validatable discovery of a universal principle, such as a universal physical principle. It is the increase of mankind's power in and over the universe, through the applications of minds cultivated in a relevant accumulation of mastery of these validatable principles, which is the only source of mankind's increased physical-economic productivity. That is the only source of true economic growth, the only source of true, physical-economic profit.

Thus, it is the private entrepreneur, functioning as a master of the work of machine-tool design, working closely with the frontiers of scientific progress in universities, who typifies the quality of entrepreneur of the most crucial importance for the success of an economy organized according to what Hamilton, among others, defined as the American System of political-economy.

As I have indicated in earlier locations, the picture of the connection among the "dots" of physical-economic progress, is by no means the linear connection superstitiously adopted as Euclidean geometry, or arithmetic. The connection assumes the geometric forms of a Gauss-Riemann hypergeometry, or what Riemann defined otherwise as his notion of a multiply-connected manifold among validated universal physical principles. The connection defined by such a manifold is a regular form of non-constant curvature, in other words, an axiomatically non-linear curvature. But, that as such is a subject for another place on another day. It is sufficient that you know that those who call themselves mathematicians, or mathematical physicists, and who propose to "connect the dots" in a linear way, as von Neumann did, are not dwelling in the real universe.

What is to be stressed here, at this point, is the following.

The relationship among money-prices is in no way congruent with the relations among real elements of the processes of physical-economy. It is not the supermarket which produces the milk, it is the farmer. The attempt to deduce milk from a theory of supermarket prices, is the behavior of a certifiable lunatic.

Similarly, the assumption, by the followers of professed satanist Bernard de Mandeville and Friedrich von Hayek's Mont Pelerin Society, of the existence of an "invisible hand" of evil mysteriously generating the benefit of a "magic of the marketplace," is the religious worship better suited to be performed by witches, not a representation of the processes of cause and effect in the real world. The only "invisible hand" which should concern you, is Wall Street's hand hidden in your pocket.

If you wish to have something which works as intended, design, build, and operate it to do so. The same principle applies to national economies. The difference between a building or a highway, on the one side, and an economy, on the other, is that the performance of an economy depends upon the cultivation of those cognitive powers of the individual human mind, by means of which mankind discovers not only experimentally validatable universal physical principles, but those Classical-artistic and related principles of statecraft, by means of which a society does what no manufactured object, nor lower form of life can do, make those discoveries of universal principle, by means of which mankind's power in, and over the universe is increased to such included effects as generating a genuine physical-economic profit.

It is building the protectionist policies of the American System of political-economy, around this principled conception of the unique contributions supplied by a suitably cultivated form of the individual human mind, which is the best existing known principle governing the way a successful form of economy works. That is something an immoral swine like John Locke, or a deranged positivist like John von Neumann, could never accept. We better accept it; we have reached the point, that that is the only premise upon which our nation, this civilization, might survive the great financial collapse which is descending upon us all now.

First published in EIR, *July 30, 1999.*

SCHILLER INSTITUTE REPORT

The New Silk Road Becomes the World Land-Bridge   VOLUME II

A Shared Future for Humanity

Introduction by Helga Zepp-LaRouche

June 20—The Executive Intelligence Review *is pleased to present here the introduction to the new volume, which is expected to be published by the end of this month.*

The "Spirit of the New Silk Road" has changed the world for the better much more thoroughly than the trans-Atlantic sector has even remotely understood until now. Since Chinese President Xi Jinping placed the New Silk Road on the agenda in September 2013 in Kazakhstan, optimism on an unprecedented scale has swept over the developing countries in particular, a sense that poverty and underdevelopment can be overcome in the foreseeable future thanks to Chinese investments in infrastructure, industry, and agriculture. Geopolitically-oriented circles in the West have not understood that China is implementing a new model of international policy, which tackles the deficit which the legacy of colonialism and imperialism has bequeathed up to this day: the absolute lack of development. And because China is thus addressing the existential needs of billions of people, that policy is likely to be the greatest revolution in the history of mankind.

In the nearly four years that have elapsed since the release of the first 374-page comprehensive study, *The New Silk Road Becomes the World Land-Bridge* in December 2014, numerous projects that were conceptualized in that report have been carried out. Others, such as the Transaqua Project for the revitalization of Lake Chad and the development of a waterway system for 12 African countries, have been agreed upon by the governments involved and feasibility studies are being drawn up. Since then, the World Land-Bridge report has been published in English, Chinese, Arabic, and German, and a Korean version will soon be available.

China's Belt and Road Initiative has become the largest infrastructure program in human history. The "Belt and Road Forum" in May 2017 brought together 29 heads of state and government and more than 1,200 representatives from more than 140 nations, including this author (see articles on Schiller Institute activities later in this report). Hundreds of conferences and seminars on this subject have been held around the world, and more and more countries see that their economic opportunities lie in becoming a hub for the New Silk Road and the "Maritime Silk Road for the 21st Century." However, it is not only the enormous economic perspectives derived from economic cooperation on a win-win basis that have fundamentally changed the overall strategic situation, but also and above all Xi Jinping's idea of a "community of shared future for mankind."

What most people in the West can no longer even imagine, is that in Xi Jinping, a statesman has assumed the political leadership of the most populous nation in the world, who is also a profound philosopher. In his opening remarks to the welcoming banquet of this year's annual conference of the Shanghai Cooperation Organization (SCO), Xi invoked the spirit of Confucius, who was born in Shandong Province, the site of the summit. Shandong was the birthplace of Confucianism, an integral part of Chinese civilization, he said, and that a just cause should be pursued for the common good, for the harmony, unity, and shared community of all nations. The future of the SCO, Xi implied, should be inspired by the spirit of Confucius! In Europe, one would have to go back at least as far as Adenauer and de Gaulle, Bismarck, and vom Stein to find a statesman who has based his policy on humanist philosophers.

With the Silk Road initiative and the idea of a community of shared future for mankind, Xi Jinping has developed a totally new model for relations among the nations of the world, which supersedes the previous geopolitical rivalries of the blocs with the higher idea of one single mankind, whose sovereign states cooperate with one another to their mutual benefit. As Xi Jinping explained in his October 18, 2017 report to the 19th National Congress of the Communist Party of China, he is pursuing the vision of initiating developments that allow for the peaceful coexistence of all sovereign nations on Earth and a happy life for all peoples by 2050.

Largely unnoticed or disregarded by the Euro-centric or America-centric view of the mainstream media, is the fact that entirely new strategic orientations are developing in Asia as a result of this grand design, and that Asian countries are in the process of overcoming past historical antagonisms and are instead working out a new type of cooperation. Numerous countries, which were played against each other until recently in geopolitical scenarios, now see a much more promising perspective in a strategic realignment of cooperation for mutual benefit and for a higher idea of the common development of all of mankind.

The historical breakthrough that President Trump and Chairman Kim Jung-un were able to achieve in Singapore on June 12, involving an agreement on full nuclear disarmament in return for security guarantees—which China wants to help provide, as well as on the lifting of sanctions and a commitment to North Korea's economic development, would have been unthinkable without the "Spirit of the New Silk Road" that has triggered throughout Asia an optimistic mindset that genuine changes for the better are indeed possible. Trump's announcement that he would end the provocative joint military maneuvers with South Korea is an important step on the road to a peace treaty between the two Koreas. Laying the ground for this development, there was intensive cooperation among South Korea, China, Russia, India, and the United States, which could become a model for solving regional conflicts.

The economic modernization pledged by the United States, Russia, and China, which will make North Korea "prosperous and wealthy," corresponds to the intention discussed at the inter-Korean summit between President Moon Jae-in and Chairman Kim Jong-un in April, and prior to that, at the Eastern Economic Forum in Vladivostok in September 2017. Both Koreas are to be included in the integration of the Belt and Road Initiative and the Eurasian Economic Union (EAEU), including the connection of a future trans-Korean railway to the Trans-Siberian Railway and to China's transportation network.

Another good example of this is the policy change in Japan and India. The Obama Administration's "Asia Pivot" was aimed at lining up countries in the Pacific region—Australia, Japan, New Zealand, and India—under the banner of an "Indo-Pacific" policy, against China and above all against the dynamic of the New Silk Road. The United States and the European Union (EU) played the India card in particular, arguing that the "world's largest democracy" (India) should cooperate with the democratic West against the authoritarian China. However, following a two-day summit between President Xi Jinping and Prime Minister Narendra Modi in April of this year, the two most populous states in the world, recalibrated their relations positively to each other. Speaking at the Shangri-La Dialogue in Singapore on June 1, Modi appealed to the world to rise above divisions and rivalries, and to opt instead to work together. He referred to the deep conceptions of Vedanta philosophy, going back to the Vedas and Upanishads of ancient India, namely, the idea of the "essential oneness of all," and the idea that every individual soul is that Being in full, and not part of that Being.

On the special relationship to China, Prime Minister Modi stressed that "No other relationship of India has as many layers as our relations with China. Our cooperation is expanding, trade is growing.... I firmly believe that Asia, and the world, will have a better future when India and China work together in trust and confidence, sensitive to each other's interests."

Modi concluded: "This world is at a crossroad. There are temptations of the worst lessons of history. But, there is also a path of wisdom. It summons us to a higher purpose: to rise above a narrow view of our interests and recognize that each of us can serve our interests better when we work together as equals in the larger good of all nations. I am here to urge all to take that path."

What is also missing from the radar screen of Western media and politicians is the change in policy in Japan. In the past, Japan was largely an integral part of the "Washington Consensus." But in recent years,

Prime Minister Shinzo Abe has expanded his relations with Russia in a number of ways, while the perspective of joint economic development of the four South Kuril Islands claimed by Japan and of the improvement of bilateral relations has raised the possibility that a peace treaty could be signed between the two countries before Abe leaves office. At the same time, Japan's skepticism toward China and the Belt and Road Initiative has given way to a positive attitude. After Abe sent Toshihiro Nikai, the Secretary General of the ruling Liberal Democratic Party, as his personal envoy to the May 2017 Belt and Road Forum, Japan shifted to full cooperation with the New Silk Road policy as of June 2017. Moreover, Abe was also the first head of government to visit the newly elected Donald Trump in Trump Tower on November 17, 2016, and then on February 10, 2017 in Washington, and after that at Mar-a Lago and that at a time when the trans-Atlantic neo-liberals were still in a state of shock over Trump's election victory.

Perhaps the most important question for the future of the world is what relationship the United States will seek toward a rising China, in order to avoid the notorious Thucydides trap. The Chinese Ambassador to the United States Cui Tiankai said in a speech in New York that there have been 16 cases in history in which an ascending power surpassed the hitherto dominant power—in 12 of those cases, it led to war, and in 4 cases, the rising power overtook the previously leading power. China, of course, does not want to go to war, the Ambassador said, and it also does not want to overtake the United States as the world superpower, but it does seek win-win cooperation on a partnership basis. To that purpose, Xi Jinping has developed a new model for relations among major powers based on the principles of absolute respect for the sovereignty of others, of non-interference in each other's internal affairs, and respect for each other's political and social system.

From this standpoint, it is most fortunate that President Trump and President Xi, from the very first visit of the latter to Mar-a Lago in April 2017 established an exceptionally friendly relationship with one another. Xi returned the invitation to Trump's private residence with a "state visit plus" for Trump during his state visit to China in November 8-10, 2017. He also reserved the Forbidden City for an entire day for a personal tour for the U.S. President and First Lady Melania Trump. Despite all the tensions with China over differences of opinion as to how to overcome the trade deficit, Trump

has repeatedly called Xi, my good friend. But it is above all the historic breakthrough with North Korea that would have simply been unthinkable without the relationship between Donald Trump and Xi Jinping.

However, while the populations of North and South Korea are enthusiastically viewing the common future now opening up, and while a completely new optimistic spirit is spreading throughout Asia, Africa, Latin America, and many countries in Eastern and Southern Europe, the mainstream media and many think-tanks and politicians are reacting to these fantastic strategic changes with such a negative attitude than one could assume that they are in a different universe. The rather special *Der Spiegel* journalist Roland Nelles described the day of the summit in Singapore as "bizarre" and the meeting of the two Presidents as "weird," which does less justice to the occasion than it affords a certain insight into Mr. Nelles' intellectual life.

For the West, it is evidently extremely difficult to grasp the new paradigm, which has developed out of the dynamic of the New Silk Road. Trapped in the old paradigm of geopolitical divisions and competition in the world, they can only see projections of their own intentions through such spectacles. From the standpoint of geopolitics, politics can only be a zero sum game—if one wins, the other must necessarily lose. They view Xi Jinping's concept of win-win cooperation with mistrust, as if it were impossible for a government to not only defend the common good of its own population, but also that of other cooperating nations.

In that respect, at the very latest, the comparison of the fiasco of the G-7 summit in Canada with the tremendous success of the simultaneous summit of the Shanghai Corporation Organization should have provided the occasion for self-critical questions about the reasons for such a difference. The multifaceted erosion of the EU is not due to any alleged interference by Russian President Vladimir Putin, but to the lack of a policy that gives equal consideration to the interests of all member states. When a certain EU Commissioner, Günther Oettinger, after the election in Italy, threatens that the markets would teach the Italians how to vote, one should not be surprised at the anger of the Italians and other Southern European populations over the effects on them of Germany's "market-compliant democracy."

The mainstream media and most of the Western think-tanks had virtually ignored the groundbreaking dynamic of the New Silk Road for some four years, but then strangely enough, a few months ago, the Australian secret services, the geopolitically-minded U.S. think-tanks CSIS and CFR, the Soros-financed European Council on Foreign Relations, and the German think-tank MERICS all launched, as if on cue, an attack on China's New Silk Road policy as allegedly imperialistic.

The combination of non-reporting and ideological, manipulative characterizations makes it difficult for ordinary entrepreneurs or citizens to have a clear picture of the historically unprecedented potential that co-operation in this initiative opens up for the European and American economies. The events of the past months and weeks should prompt us to reflect on the now undeniable inherent weaknesses of the neo-liberal model of globalization, and to revive the strengths of the best traditions of the West in our cooperation with China, and to develop a common model for shaping the future.

The world is changing dramatically and the change is happening in Asia. President Xi Jinping, as we mentioned, opened this year's summit of the Shanghai Cooperation Organization in Qingdao with a reference to the thinking of Confucius which should inspire the future of the organization. And indeed, Chinese Foreign Minister Wang Yi's remarks at the final press conference of the SCO summit reflected the spirit of Confucius: the SCO is building a new world order, he said, based on mutual trust, mutual benefit, equality, respect for the diversity and common development of civilizations. Its intention, he explained, is to transcend such outdated concepts such as the clash of civilizations, the Cold War, and thinking in the geometry of zero-sum games or exclusionary clubs.

The new era must be based on the best traditions of all the cultures involved. In China, Confucius stands for the ideal of self-perfection through life-long learning and ennoblement of the character as a pre-condition for harmonious coexistence in the family, the nation, and among nations. And the notion of the "mandate of Heaven" implies that the duty of government is to ensure the common good. In Indian culture, this corresponds in principle to the concept of Dharma, the idea that universal laws set the rules for shaping relations on Earth, i.e., that the cosmic order is also valid on Earth. The five principles of the Pancheel Treaty and the concept of Ahimsa are culturally specific, and yet represent ideas that correspond to a positive image of man as the basis for the political order.

For European civilization, which America belongs to, the equivalent is the humanist tradition. An expression of this approach are the ideas of Nicholas of Cusa, the *coincidentia oppositorum*, that is, that human reason is capable of a higher level of thinking, on which the contradictions of the intellect are resolved. Order in the macrocosm is only possible if all the microcosms develop in the best possible way and to their mutual benefit. The 1648 Treaty of Westphalia is built on this foundation, which gave rise to international law, as is the philosophy of Gottfried Wilhelm Leibniz and Friedrich Schiller. In Russia, the same basic principle is expressed in the idea of Vladimir Vernadsky, that the significance of the Noösphere is constantly increasing over that of the biosphere, and that therefore the role of creative reason as a physical power increases.

The spirit of a new beginning, the cultural optimism about imminent breakthroughs in fundamental research, and an unprecedented dynamic toward the betterment of mankind's living conditions—all this characterizes the development in Asia, and this optimism has long since "rubbed off" on Latin America and Africa. We in Europe and the United States should recognize and exploit the tremendous potential it will mean for our economies if we join in this win-win cooperation. Provided we count on qualitative innovation as a source of social wealth, collaboration with the New Silk Road is by no means a threat; on the contrary, it offers us the urgently needed chance to re-discover our true identity.